M000211707

NAMASlay

THE SAVVY SOULPRENEUR

NAMASlay

LIVING RICH: WISDOM FROM
HEART-CENTERED BOSS BABES

Star House
PUBLISHING

COLLECTED BY CAROL STARR TAYLOR

LISA CARTER • JULIE CRYNS • PATI DIAZ • DAWN ESPINOZA • ANNA GASPARI
JAMIE GATES • CHRISTINE HENDERSON • SANDRA LISI • DR. KIM REDMAN
MICHELE MAHER • MALI PHONPADITH • ANNA ZECCOLO REEVES

© 2022 Star House Publishing Inc.

The Savvy Soulpreneur: Namaslay

Published by Star House Publishing Inc.

All rights reserved.

This book may not be reproduced, in whole or in part, in any form or by any electronic or mechanical means, or the facilitation thereof, including recording, photocopying, scanning, or by information storage and retrieval systems, without permission in writing from the publisher. Except by a reviewer, who may quote brief passages in a review.

The views and opinions expressed are those of the authors. Before using any advice in this book, please consult and use the recommendations of your physician or regular mental wellness or healthcare provider. Although the authors and publisher have made every effort to make sure all information is correct at press time, the authors and publisher do not assume and hereby disclaim any liability to any party for any loss, damage, disruptions caused by stories with this book, whether such information is a result of errors or emission, accident, slander, or other cause.

For any information regarding permission and bulk purchases contact:

www.starhousepublishing.com or email
info@starhousepublishing.com

ISBN PAPERBACK   978-1-989535-57-8
ISBN HARDCOVER   978-1-989535-58-5
ISBN E-BOOK   978-1-989535-59-2

Printed in the United States of America
First Edition, 2022.

Design by: Susi Clark | Creative Blueprint Design
Edited by: Akosua (Jackie) Brown

CONTENTS

You are allowed to be both a masterpiece
and a work in progress simultaneously.

Sophia Bush

Lisa Carter

Lisa Carter is a multi-published author with her first publication in The Soulology Chronicles: GRIT, Reiki Master, certified Life Coach, and has added Real Estate Agent to her professional credentials. After twenty-eight years, she left her corporate career behind. Lisa is passionate about helping others and making a difference.

The Boss Of Me

Lisa Carter

*She remembered who she was
and the game changed.*
Lalah Deliah

Due to living with alcoholics, my childhood was a bit chaotic.
I am pretty sure this is why I always wanted to work and make
my own money. For a variety of reasons, home life being a major
one, I ended up quitting school in tenth grade. I didn't really
think it through—I just stopped going to school and continued
to work. I tried to go back to high school the following year,
but it resulted in the same outcome. There were many external
upheavals in my family that I was unable to control: I couldn't
focus. The only thing I could control was me going to work.
The decision to drop out—not once but twice—affected me my
entire life, both personally and professionally.

Not Good Enough

At the age of nineteen, while moving in with a person I thought was my savior, I decided that I was ready to go back to school and registered at a local college. The plan was to get my GED equivalency and then a degree. I was so excited to do it and felt ready. I even met a friend who was embarking on the same adventure as me. We started classes together, and things were going well. I was thoroughly enjoying college life. We carpooled and made a few other friends. My live-in boyfriend manipulated me, begging me to spend more time with him and sabotaging my attempts to study or go to class. At the time, I didn't realize this was what was happening, and it led to me dropping out of the GED program a few months later. I felt torn, lost, and out of control, yet again. Looking back now, I realized that my soon-to-be husband was a narcissist and he was calling the shots. This was just the beginning of it.

When I was twenty-one, we got married and moved to the suburbs. Over the next five years, we had three children. I took several courses while the kids were young, as it still haunted me that I didn't have an education, meaning a degree. It bothered me so much that I started to compare myself to those who did have one and I put them in a much higher category of worth than my own. I would even go so far as to wonder why these moms would hang out with me, because they had university education and I did not. For many years, this was the question I tortured myself with. At this time, I was less conscious of my limiting beliefs, lack of self-worth, and budding imposter syndrome.

Although I chose this life—marriage and children who were my life and my *"big why"*—I didn't feel accomplished. My husband reminded me of how inadequate I was intellectually and educationally. I didn't fight it because it just validated my existing thoughts of, *"You don't have an education. You aren't smart. No one will ever think you are good enough. I am not good enough."*

First Steps To Power

I knew I had to get out of the marriage, but how? I worked part-time, had no education, and would never be able to support me and my children, or so I thought. This conversation replayed in my head constantly and that is what kept me in that marriage for far too long. However, one day I woke up. Something inside me snapped. I realized that I needed to take my power back and felt that I had no choice but to leave: I was not in a safe place and neither were my children. I had no clue how I was going to do this, but I knew I would. Somehow, some way.

A year later, a friend recommended me for a job at his place of employment. The job was on the order-taking desk of the customer service department. The night before the interview, I couldn't sleep. This was a full-time job, benefits, holidays, and sick days. I had a lot of anxiety because this was too important for me and my children's future to mess up. I worried because this position asked for a college education to start. As much as I knew, I had to get this job, I was petrified they were going to realize that I had no education, that I didn't belong there.

The next morning, I went to the interview, afraid they would suspect immediately just by looking at me that I was *"less than"* because I didn't have the college education they wanted. What was I going to do if they asked me about a college degree, my experiences, or about anything? As my only recent jobs were part-time and I was now a single mother of three, I felt desperate. I *needed* to get this job. I drove myself insane with the *"what if's"* and overthinking but I was focused to survive. I felt empowered in one way, although I didn't have a *formal* education. What *I did have* was the ability to communicate and present myself professionally. So, I went in with my head held high, took a deep breath and summoned up my courage to enter that interview *like the boss babe I wanted to be.* Not only did I kill that interview, but they also hired me on the spot.

Navigating The Corporate World

I started my new position the following week, every day thinking someone was going to figure out I didn't belong there or that I wasn't good enough. The thought that I didn't have an education would not leave me alone. Over the next few years, with our office position being unionized, I was lucky enough to move around into a few lateral positions, gaining experience in customer service, accounting, and logistics. Somehow, I was lucky enough to catch on quickly within each role. But was it luck? I worked very hard to quickly learn each new position I obtained, and even studied at night, as I was so afraid.

After about two years in, I was voted in as the union steward backup for my office. I put myself up for the role for the sole purpose of protecting my job: I knew union stewards were the last to be laid off. With a few company mergers going on, layoffs were looking inevitable. I happened to be voted in just prior to negotiating our new contracts for the transforming company. This was a whole new world of learning for me. But I *was sure* there was no way I was going to be able to sit in a room with senior managers and head union reps without being discovered that I didn't belong there. Once again, I set my fears aside and moved forward. By this point, I was the sole provider in every aspect for me and my children.

Before negotiations started, I sat every night and read the entire union book making notes and identifying so many things that made zero sense to me; however, my thoughts were more aligned with management than that of the union mindset. As we all sat in a room—there were ten to twelve of us—going through the contract item by item, I sat back quietly, afraid to speak up or draw attention to myself. As items were being tabled that I had an opinion on, I could no longer remain quiet: I had to voice my opinion. Over the next weeks, we were able to be aligned on making some significant improvements in the office. We also were able to update some of the items that appeared outdated and had just rolled over from contract to contract.

Putting my fears aside, I started to participate in our negotiations and to voice my opinions more and more frequently. I had input on many items, some aligning with management and others with the union. The biggest change that was made was that employees could no longer move into open positions based on seniority alone. They needed to meet basic qualifications. The company agreed to set up inhouse training for all existing employees to bring them to the *"basic"* level needed. All new hires would have to meet the same qualifications to be hired. Imagine me with zero qualifications, thinking this was a good idea; however, at the time, it made sense to me.

As I was the one who brought forth this change, to help make it possible, I was assigned to work directly with our HR Training Manager, Diana. Using a third-party company, we were to determine the qualification levels for each position. Wow, what an opportunity! Not only was I excited about the additional learnings that came with this, but I also thought as long as I was part of the training, I would be excluded from any testing. Genius! Or so, I thought.

Diana set up an appointment for us to meet with a company for us to review their assessment and training process, along with the different options available to get everyone trained. What I wasn't aware of was that Diana had set us both up to participate in a day of doing the assessments and quizzes, rather than just viewing others do them. What? I was with one of the smartest women I think I have ever met, and I was to do this alongside her? I felt sick. She would see my results and change her perception about me. The entire assessment was a variety of aptitude type questions and quizzes ranging all over the place. To my surprise, I scored well. Very well.

Moving On Up

The following year, the big merger resulted in a split in the company, and I landed on the non-unionized side of the corporation. A position as a supervisor came up in my department, and I knew I had to get it. It was more money, more responsibility, and involved managing people—none of which I had any experience in. I used my new work experiences to sell myself. I focused on my kids, and living in survival mode. Once again, I knocked this interview out of the park and got the job.

I decided it was time to start creating the life I have always wanted. First step, get my GED. The next week, I went to the continuing education office, and immediately signed up. After six weeks of upgrading and refresher classes, I wrote my exam. I passed.

My learning continued. In addition to nightly college classes, I continued to look for every opportunity I could to increase my resume education section. When one wasn't present, I created them and would bring ideas to my boss or HR. This allowed me to take courses covered through work, and many times I got approved to take them during work hours. It was already difficult enough being a single parent and keeping up with the active schedules of three children. And I'd always felt that this job was my *"now"* job: what I had to do, not what I wanted to do. The truth was, I never really had the opportunity to figure out what it really was I wanted to do, so I made the best of it.

Even with all this experience, in the corporate world, I still felt that I was an imposter, that I was *"less than."* How did I manage to give that *one little piece of paper* I never got so much power? To top it off, after devoting fourteen years to my job, my position was eliminated.

I still remember driving home that day looking out my sunroof and saying, *"Ok God, I guess you have a plan for me."* The truth is I was exhausted. I didn't have time to let the fear of the unknown creep in yet. The year prior, I'd had thyroid cancer and

I still was not fully recovered physically or mentally. I had been raising three kids alone, working constantly, plus volunteering. I had not stopped in fourteen years.

The following morning, I got up and it was strange not having anywhere to go. My life had been halted. I did not want to go back to a corporate job but was not in a position to do anything else. I did end up working in the corporate world for the next nine years. By then I had truly had enough.

Throughout those nine years, to supplement my corporate income, I decided to do something fun, just for me. I got involved in direct sales and immediately it took off. I was soaring. Then I fell. Staying with it but coasting for years, I realized why I didn't work harder at it. It was because a new fear developed. A fear of success. As soon as I started to see any success in direct sales, I froze. I realize now that I was my own saboteur. I watched everyone around me succeed and everyone was telling me that I had everything going for me. I just didn't believe in myself. I dropped it and felt like a failure.

The World Stopped

I realized something about myself, finally. My life was about control: being controlled, lack of control, and grasping for control. One thing that couldn't be predicted, was when the world shut down with a global pandemic in March 2020. COVID-19.

As someone who spent over forty years working and fighting, the lack of control when the pandemic hit, sent me in a frozen tailspin. Turning fifty-five, hit me too, it was a big deal. Those *"Freedom 55"* insurance commercials from childhood swirled in my head. I thought it was that *"magical"* age that we were all supposed to *"have it all together,"* and be ready to *"retire and enjoy life,"* didn't help. I had finally felt worthy, until I didn't. I had planned on taking a real estate course, and instead of studying, I found myself glued to the TV, watching the news, series reruns, and became best friends with cabernet.

I was avoiding the real estate course books sitting on my table. That old narrative that I couldn't learn, the fear of failing again and also the fear of success crept back into my mind. Excuses were playing endlessly in my mind. I also felt I was letting not only myself down, but my daughter who I was planning to work with by joining her real estate team.

I realize now that I was also using the *"I can't study a formal course"* as an excuse because I was fearful of joining my already successful daughter and basically working under her well-established brand. I felt an uncertainty with the role reversal. Me being *"the mom,"* joining my daughter's business with her work ethic and structure. I ruminated over the thoughts of, *"I'm fifty-five, can I really do this and start again?"* *"What would the dynamics be like? How would I fit in wearing this new hat in our relationship?"* However, with my mindset shift and desire to succeed in the real estate industry, I welcomed the opportunity to learn from my daughter, who not only did I trust implicitly, but is an expert in her field.

It was then that I made a conscious decision to use my fear as a driving force to snap me out of my comfort zone. It was time to use the world pause to my advantage and to stop wasting time. I realized that I only had myself to rely on, so I had two choices: go back to the corporate world which I didn't want to do or push through and slay those real estate books and get my license.

The first step to manifesting my dream life was being given the key to the office I would be working in as a self-employed real estate agent. I used that office to study for the test and felt the energy of the office.

Journey To Wisdom

One of the key lessons I have learned, is that the skills we acquire along the way can be interchangeable; for example, a skill gained through work experience is just as valid as one gained through education. We are not to be defined by our pasts, our education, or even our financial status. The shift from being in a long corporate career to an entrepreneur takes a lot of consistent hard work, with many days of planting seeds that may or may not take root.

As an entrepreneur, there are many twists and turns even in a day. I have come to discover that it is based on personal effort, mindset, the belief in ourselves and trust in the Universe that makes things all work as they should. It took me a long time to figure that out. Looking back now at all of the skills I developed throughout my career, I now believe that they are just as valid as those obtained from a degree.

Since I have passed all of the exams and work as a licensed real estate agent, I truly value my experience *even more* than that of a university degree that I had so desperately wanted all of these years. I understand that although I don't have a diploma or degree, I do have many courses, certifications and lessons in my *"tool box."*

LESSON 1:
The Definition of Success

Success is different for everyone. My idea of success is when you have achieved what you set out to achieve. I have now created a life that truly makes me happy and excited to get up each and every day.

LESSON 2:
Mindset, Pivot, and Shift

Looking back throughout the years at the different jobs and experiences I have had has allowed me to grow and develop. I have always tried to take any negative experiences and turn them into a positive learning lesson. Finding the positive in every situation or lesson is not always easy; but, if you can develop that skill, you will be much better for it.

LESSON 3:
Changing Careers

Changing careers can cause a multitude of feelings: I felt bold, scared and exhilarated all at the same time. Get rid of the fears and the what if's and just do it. Life is too short to be unhappy every day. I still work hard, actually harder most days, only now I control my hours and my pay. *I Am The Boss of Me.*

LESSON 4:
We Are Our Own Worst Enemies

We are all different, unique, and fabulous. Do not let someone else's insecurities, or your own fears, tell you any different. Talk nice to yourself using kind and positive words. You are enough.

LESSON 5:
The Corporate World vs Entrepreneurship

In the corporate world, typically it will be your boss who will dictate your pay increases, your hours, and workload. They will determine your success, not you. Whereas, being an entrepreneur, you get paid on the commitment level and hours you put into building your own business. Your success level will be determined by the amount of support and repeat business you get.

LESSON 6:
Labels

Applying labels to yourself or to others will stunt your growth and developments. You will become what you hear the most. Be kind always.

LESSON 7:
We Are Here To Serve

Real estate as with every business is about people: helping people, building relationships, listening, empathy, compassion, problem solving, and caring. If you are in it for money only, your business will be short lived. When you truly care and are passionate about what you are doing, the money will follow.

LESSON 8:
Be Persistent and Consistent

One of the pivotal lessons I have learned, and one that keeps me going is that each and every day that I show up and am consistent and persistent, I make a difference in the lives of others, including my own.

The Boss Of Me

I have relished in the roll up the sleeves entrepreneurial spirit and the *"if it's meant to be, it's up to me"* mindset. Although there were fears, many fears tied into this especially with the ups and downs of financial uncertainty, I pushed through, passed my exams, and am doing something I love.

Not only have I proved I can do anything to myself, but also to my children and grandchildren. This means the world to me as my family was my *"big why"* when I had to survive. Now that I am thriving, they *still* remain my *"why."* I wanted them to see that nothing is impossible at any age. The imposter syndrome has been annihilated. At age, fifty-eight, I have proven to myself that I am not only worthy but that I can become and overcome any and all obstacles in my way. What I have learned is that mindset is everything. We create the narrative both positively and negatively. I know now that my journey has taken me here to my purpose and where I was destined to be. The boss of me.

Your life will be transformed when you make peace with your shadow.
The caterpillar will become a breathtakingly beautiful butterfly.
You will no longer have to pretend to be someone you're not.
You will no longer have to prove you're good enough.
When you embrace your shadow you will no longer have to live in fear.
Find the gifts of your shadow and you will finally revel
in all the glory of your true self.
Then you will have the freedom to create the life
you have always desired.

Debbie Ford

Julie Cryns

Julie Cryns is the owner at Julie Cryns Grief Services. After her husband died in 2011, she felt drawn to work with people in grief, as well as those facing end of life. She holds certifications in Grief Education, Grief Literacy, and Supporting Grieving Children, as well as End of Life Doula Training. She feels honored to work as a Grief Coach, Grief Educator, and Grief Advocate in Newmarket, Ontario.

Heart And Soul

Julie Cryns

You don't have to see the whole
staircase to take the first step.

Martin Luther King

Almost a decade after my husband died, my life took another un-planned and unscripted turn. At age fifty-three, I decided to take a leap of faith—I gave up the financial security of a comfortable teaching salary to start my own business as a death doula.

The run-up to my decision reminded me of the year 2006 when my husband Mark was first diagnosed with leukemia. I remember the overwhelming sense of grief, which threatened to engulf me, and how ill-equipped to deal with it I felt. Our children were only two and four years old and I had very limited family support in this country. I felt very alone and fearful of what lay ahead. I worried about the possibility of my kids growing up without a dad and, in the meantime, I had to start juggling the responsibilities of a wife, mother, and caregiver.

Very soon, the daily grind of medications and appointment waiting rooms became a blur, and my frustration and anxiety threatened to eat me alive. I felt powerless to help or prevent things from becoming worse, and I had to do something with all my nervous energy. I needed to find something good that would enable me to make sense of a painful situation. This is a lesson that I often share with my grief clients today. Even in the darkest of times, by focusing our attention on the *good*, we can learn to take control over the things which are still within our control. For example, we can *choose* to notice a beautiful sunset or appreciate the benefits of living in a country with an advanced healthcare system. We have the ability to choose where we focus our attention, and this, I have learned, is a key to resilient grieving.

A Moment Of Clarity

While driving in my car, on the long daily drive to the hospital where Mark was an inpatient, I realized that I needed to take control over whatever I could, knowing that much of our life at that point was totally beyond my control. I needed to find an opportunity which would enable me to get back in the driving seat, rather than being a passive observer. Before I parked the car that day, I was working on a vision of a local, outdoor, family event, which would honor Mark's journey and raise funds for research into this brutal disease. I was already aware that leukemia is probably *the* most common of childhood cancers, so I decided this would be a great use of my time and energy. I named our event the *"Mad Hatter's Walk for Leukemia Research,"* since Mark had lost his hair to chemotherapy and he loved to joke around with different hats and wigs to make our kids laugh. Planning and coordinating the first walk gave me something to focus on, and it was a welcome distraction for my husband. As a graphic designer, he created a beautiful logo and designed flyers for us to distribute.

Although I had very little experience of planning and coordinating big public events, I soon discovered that both passion and determination together create a superpower. The first annual *Mad Hatter's Walk* became a reality in May 2007, ten months after Mark's diagnosis. We had over four hundred participants, corporate sponsors, a live band, a silent auction, a bagpiper to lead the walk, golf carts for those unable to walk, and a picnic lunch. My parents flew in from Scotland, and Mark's doctors drove up from the city. It was a bright light in an otherwise dark and depressing time, and it helped to give us a sense of purpose which would help us to get through the following year. Over the course of three years, we raised an incredible $120,000 for leukemia research, and it felt good to be playing an active role in our journey.

Relapse

Remission came and went and, in the fall of 2010, Mark relapsed. This called for a different protocol that included three chemo injections into the spine. Sadly, Mark reacted to the drug immediately after the final injection and it caused him severe brain damage. During this time, I became very frustrated with my husband's healthcare team. Communication between Mark's healthcare teams was poor, and my questions were often met with contradictory answers. They assured me that the brain damage would not be permanent, and they qualified this by saying that it could take some time to heal.

Once again, I found myself trying to coordinate events for which I had no prior experience. Mark was taken off the bone marrow donor list and transferred back to our local hospital where the physio team did their very best to teach him to walk again, but any progress never lasted.

Since Mark was no longer able to speak or tend to his own personal care, and the local hospital unit was unable to support him effectively, I decided to bring him home. Even in this, I had to put pressure on them to discharge him. They advocated that he be put into a long-term care facility as I would not be able to cope at home. However, I refused to accept this as a solution, and they accepted my decision.

I felt scared about how we would manage at home, but I knew I could not allow him to spend whatever time he had left in a long-term care facility. He was forty-nine years old and he had full cognitive capacity so I brought him home and we adapted.

Last Moments

In mid-June 2011, I received a phone call from the doctor. The cancer was back and Mark would most likely die within three weeks. It was my job to tell him, our children, and the rest of the family. This was the hardest thing I had ever had to do, but I was learning that I could do hard things. Three weeks, however, turned out to be only twelve days. Although Mark had wanted to die at home, when the end came near, I couldn't go through with it.

He was not conscious, and I was worried that our children's lasting memory of their dad might be a frightening or traumatic one.

I felt very unprepared for what might happen and, looking back, I wish I had had an end-of-life doula by my side to offer knowledge, comfort and support. I was also afraid that he might die while he was waiting in the hospital's emergency department surrounded by strangers. Taking matters into my own hands, I looked up *"hospice near me"* and got through to a small hospice in a nearby town the same evening. Astonishingly, they had one bedroom available, and they offered it to us.

That turned out to be Mark's last night. He died the following afternoon in the safety and peaceful surroundings of hospice. I was with him when his heart stopped beating, and I remember the feeling of disbelief. I was also breathtakingly grateful for the fact that I could spend Mark's last moments with him in such a warm and peaceful environment. I wondered if, had life turned out differently, I could have found work and meaning in such a place. However, I returned to teaching and lived on autopilot for several years, learning to deal with the challenges of being a working mother and a single parent of two young children.

Looking back, I realize that I could have handled my children's grief more effectively, but instead I followed the path that most bereaved partners take. I distracted them with treats, trips, and fun activities. Nowadays, I understand that I could have offered them more space to grieve. I could have given them opportunities to ask questions and figure out what they had learned about themselves from the experience. It is only now that I have trained as a Grief Educator, with a specialty in supporting grieving children, that

I realize I could have done it differently. Of course, I was also grieving, so it was never going to be straightforward.

Finding Purpose

Years later, while still teaching full-time, a chance encounter led me to becoming a volunteer at a recently opened hospice nearby. Spending time with hospice families reminded me why I had been drawn to this work. It made me realize that something had been missing in my life for a long time, and that was a sense of meaning. Being with families whose loved one was dying actually gave me a sense of value and purpose that I didn't even know had been missing. I understand now that this *"chance encounter"* was the nudge I needed, and I do not believe in coincidences.

What Is A Death Doula?

While still teaching full-time, I stumbled across the role of an end-of-life doula, and I was intrigued. Was it by *"chance"* that somebody mentioned the term to me? I think not. My hospice work was rewarding, but I knew I had more to offer, and this course sounded like a great fit for me.

Death doulas have been around for centuries, but the term is relatively new. Just as a birth doula coaches a mother and family through the birthing process, a death doula does likewise at the other end of life.

When I looked into the course content to earn certification, it seemed to be exactly what I was looking for. As I started my training, and connecting with other, like-minded people, I was reminded of that expression, *"You don't know what you don't know."* The more I learned, the more I wanted to know. I felt inspired.

Leap Of Faith

The fact is, death is just a part of life, but it has become primarily a *medical* event so that, when someone dies, there is a sense of failure, even discrimination. A death doula's role is to provide non-medical comfort and practical support, and also to advocate for a client's wishes. Above all, our goal is to normalize the idea of death and dying. If somebody wishes to die at home, surrounded by their family, we can help to make this possible. I also discovered that there is a community of heart-led women in Ontario, Canada who all share a passion for serving people at the end of life.

Having taken many courses to expand my knowledge further, I knew that I had chosen the right path. I decided to commit to starting a business. However, I felt deeply unprepared for this next step. I even had a dilemma about what to name my company, since I was initially looking for a name which would sound nice and perhaps had some meaning. Sadly, all the names I came up with were already taken, and, as it turns out, that was a blessing. With guidance from my incredibly helpful local small business office, I registered the business under my own name and applied for a Master Business License. Since I am a sole proprietor and I am the brand, it makes sense that the company bears my name.

There seemed to be a long list of requirements for setting up a business and, having never done this before, I made some choices I would not care to repeat. However, once I had established my company, the next step was to obtain liability insurance. After several insurance companies declined to offer me coverage, I eventually found one who had actually heard of the death doula role and was prepared to sell me a package. The next thing on my list was to address the need for a website since I felt that would add credibility to this little-known field of work.

I was completely ignorant as to how a website is created and that it also requires ongoing maintenance. I began with a homemade website, kindly made for me by my niece. Although I loved the look of it, I discovered that it wasn't working to attract business, so I reluctantly engaged a professional who was recommended by a friend. This was when I discovered that not all professional relationships are advantageous and that recommendations from friends can be problematic. This was a frustrating process, cost me thousands of dollars over a period of six months, and resulted in a website which *looked* professional but over which I had zero control.

The website developer did not allow me admin access, and when I asked what would happen to the website should he disappear off the face of the earth, he said he was not planning to do that. If I wanted to make even the slightest change, I had to pay him $150, which was his hourly rate. He then left the country and stopped responding to my emails. Fortunately for me, I met another web designer through a networking group who was able to hack into my site and migrate it to a different location and safety. My new web developer respects my vision, is patient with my endless questions, and our contract is clear. It has been a demoralizing process to get here, but I have finally found a professional with integrity. I have discovered that patience and persistence are absolutely key.

Finding My Niche

Did I make some costly mistakes in the beginning? Absolutely. I think one of my biggest mistakes was embarking on so many expensive training courses because I wanted to specialize in everything. I trained to become an End-of-Life Doula, an Advance Care Planner, a Grief Educator, and an intuitive Reiki Practitioner. I took courses in Grief Literacy, Supporting Grieving Children, and ACT (Acceptance & Commitment Therapy). I attended webinars and studied many books; after a while, I realized I was in danger of becoming an eternal student.

The truth is, there was a sense of safety and predictability involved in immersing myself in learning. I felt that I needed to be everything to everyone and wanted to be prepared for absolutely any situation I found myself in. Along with my deep desire to serve others, I wanted to reassure my clients with my knowledge and expertise across the whole spectrum of deathcare. However, I realized that you cannot be an expert in everything.

The positive outcome of completing so many certifications, was that I learned which areas of work made sense to me on a personal level. By the end of the first year, I was certified in everything from Reiki to Advance Care Planning, but the reality was that I did not feel confident or competent to offer *all* of these services. I also began to realize that I was actually diluting my perceived value. I needed to stop accumulating certificates and training, and I needed to start trusting myself and my own innate ability.

Realizing My Worth

My next big hurdle was to establish *what* to charge and *how* to charge. Since this is a comparatively new industry, and there is no governing board to dictate expectations, there really wasn't a precedent to follow. Coaching pricing is all over the map, so I asked a few friends what they would be prepared to pay, but their answers varied.

Being inexperienced and just starting out, I thought perhaps I should begin by offering my services for free. It also felt wrong to charge clients for my services at such a vulnerable and emotional time in their lives. With some help from a business coach, I worked on understanding the concept of perceived value, understanding my worth, and that what I offer is a specialization. I also needed to learn how to leverage that if I was going to run my practice as a business. Early on, it had been pointed out to me that, *"If you're not making money, it's a hobby, not a business."* This still did not sit well with me, and it took more than a year to feel confident enough to charge for my services without apology.

Death Is A Dirty Word

So, what was the greatest barrier to starting my practice, other than my pursuit of accumulating certifications? I discovered that the greatest barrier to doing this work and helping people through the process is actually the word *death* itself.

As a society, we are very uncomfortable talking about death—let alone *planning* for it—even though death is as natural as life itself. There are many who think it is bad luck, morbid, or plain bad manners to say the word, let alone discuss it. So, end-of-life planning and support was the area I initially intended to specialize in, but there is still so much reluctance to even acknowledge this momentous event, that I realized it may take much longer than I anticipated to serve in the role of a death doula.

I was acutely aware that I had spent hundreds of dollars on training to become an end-of-life doula, followed by hundreds more to gain additional skills which I thought might enhance my work. However, I became equally aware that I needed to re-evaluate my strengths and commit to following those, instead of simply accumulating more and varied certifications. I felt some guilt about the way I had plunged into all that learning, spending all sorts of money before I was even earning any income. However, the truth is, all that learning did serve a purpose. It was a great foundation for the work I do now, and it showed me that the area I feel the most compelled to serve in is that of grief support. It was a worthwhile investment.

So, I decided to focus on expanding my expertise in the area of grief. Grief is, after all, a common thread which unites us all. When someone or something we love is taken from us, we experience a grief response. It is not an emotion, as many people believe, but rather a whole-body response to loss. We don't get to decide how we will feel, or how long it will last, there is no rule book, and no precedent for us to follow. Mourning, which is the outward display of grief, often involves rituals and patterns of social behaviors, but grieving itself is a unique and fundamentally personal process.

I find myself working in the area of grief support and education much more than end-of-life support at the moment. Am

I okay with that? Absolutely. I believe that I can make a difference in both roles, and I am honored to be able to help the people who reach out to me.

Learning: What I Know Now

This journey, which for me really began sixteen years ago with my husband's cancer diagnosis, has been one of self-discovery. I have learned so much about myself, and much of it was unexpected. I didn't realize that all of my years in the classroom would be such a great foundation for my work as a grief educator. I didn't realize that planning and coordinating the *Mad Hatter's Walk* fifteen years ago would pave the way for me to create a community workshop event on Grief, Loss, & Emotional Intelligence. I didn't know that I would be embarking on a new career in my mid-fifties. I couldn't have known that the loss of my husband would be the catalyst for me to find new meaning in my life while honoring his life.

These are some of the things that I have learned through the process of building my practice:

1. When you truly believe in what you are doing, people will listen, and your business will grow. I have accepted every opportunity which has been offered to me in an effort to make my name known. I have stepped out of my comfort zone to address rooms full of strangers and answer questions in live interviews. I am a collaborative author of a book about women in heart-led businesses. I have agreed to participate in a Shop Local ad campaign for a large local

business, and I have challenged myself to carve out a space where there was not one before.

2. I have stumbled a few times, but I have learned that I can do hard things and that persistence pays off.

3. I have discovered that the road to success in business is not straight, it is often uphill, and sometimes you have to travel by night. I am active on social media, but the best way for me to grow my business has been through networking groups several times a week. Through these, I have made useful connections, presented to small groups, and answered many questions about my scope of work.

4. To acknowledge and accept my limitations and to ask for help.

5. Some business relationships are not productive and need to be ended. The resulting frustration and financial losses are just part of the learning.

6. The best way to become known is to talk to everybody and take every opportunity to share my vision and experiences.

7. I am good at what I do, and it is okay to put a monetary value on my time and expertise.

8. It is never too late to give up on an old dream, or even to create a new one. In reality, our dreams can evolve and change just like we do.

9. Above all, I have learned to trust in myself and my ability, both as a grief coach and businesswoman.

10. I feel honored to help people navigate their grief journeys, and I know I will continue to grow as my business evolves. I will never stop dreaming.

I've learned that people will forget what you said,
people will forget what you did,
but people will never forget how you made them feel.

Maya Angelou

A very important thing is not to make up
your mind that you are any one thing.

Gertrude Stein

Pati Diaz

Pati Diaz is a Latina entrepreneur, certified Manifestation Coach and Founder of Blue Moon Manifestations. Her passion is to help women uplevel their lives by letting go of old identities and unleashing their inner rock star. Pati believes that you can manifest the things, experiences, and circumstances you desire. She refers to this as Manifesting ME. Pati has workshops and also works with clients on an individual basis. Currently, Pati lives in the Los Angeles area and works with women globally.

Blue Moon Serenade: Manifesting Me

Pati Diaz

> *So imagine that the lovely moon*
> *is playing just for you — everything*
> *makes music if you really want it to.*
>
> **Giles Andreae**

We all have a vision or image of the most amazing badass version of ourselves, one we wish we could be like. Mine is a rebellious rock chick. She says and does whatever the fuck she wants and doesn't worry about whether other people get it, like it, or approve. She doesn't care about being *"appropriate"* or what other people think about her. She isn't concerned about being liked or accepted. And fitting in? Actually, she prefers not to. She wants to be a unique contribution to the overall mosaic—one of the random, awkward, and weird, though, perfectly beautiful pieces.

My journey to entrepreneurship has, in truth, been the process of realizing that *she is me*. It is one of learning how to be this version of myself instead of just *wishing* I could be her. She is not an unrealistic dream, but part of the real me: my personal lighthouse beacon, a light in the dark when I am in one of life's shit storms feeling lost and disoriented. She is the anchor that keeps me from drifting too far off course and is my lifeline back to what is important. She knows the way and is always ready to guide me. My journey to entrepreneurship is the process of manifesting me—my Inner Rock Chick. And she is a fucking star!

The Illusion Of Job Security

Both of my maternal grandparents were immigrants and became business owners who worked for themselves. My dad is an immigrant and has had several businesses. This shows me I come from a line of dreamers, visionaries, adventurers, and risk takers.

From the vantage point of looking back, the questions that arose in my mind are, *"Why does wanting better for ourselves somehow translate into following an established formula of formal, higher education that leads to an established job working for someone else?" "Why doesn't it also include the option of growing our own empire in whatever way it best suits us to achieve it?"* Is it how the message was delivered and the way we were guided that seems to exclude the paths that most attracted me? Or perhaps, it was the way we received and interpreted (and, in my case, rebelled against) the message.

I interpreted the message as working for someone else provides job security and that following the *established formula* was *the way* to do better and achieve more. Using the established formula, according to the message, eliminates so-called risk. This passed down message *is not for me.* Trying to follow the formula has shown me that job security is an illusion. I've been fired twice and even had to apply for government support when employers heavily reduced my work hours.

Early Dreams Are Clues

*Don't worry if you're making waves
just by being yourself. The moon does it all the time.*

Scott Stabile

What to do after high school? I had no clue. Well, that's not entirely true. I held two secret dreams in my eighteen-year-old heart.

The first *"way out-there"* rock star dream was to become the tour manager for rock bands. I daydreamed about turning my dad's trucking company into a transport company for all the gear and equipment as well as incorporating tour buses.

The second came from one of those, *"What Job Would You Be Good At"* tests given to me by my high school guidance counselor which indicated I should consider journalism or being a writer. Both seemed like a good fit since I won a writing contest my senior year of high school and I did consider writing as something to pursue.

What stopped me? First, was the feedback and stories saying *"That's not very steady work,"* which made it seem unsafe. Second, was the belief that the only way to achieve this was to have a college degree. I'm a great student and love learning but going to college and getting a degree was not my jam or idea of a good time.

I didn't apply to any four-year colleges or universities and did not tour or visit any college campuses (except for Cal State LA on a high school field trip). But education was important to my parents, so as a compromise, and a way to buy some time to figure out what the hell I wanted to do, I went to community college. This scenario is a perfect example of how I began a decades-long cycle of rebelling against the *"shoulds"* of life, then trying to find a way to make those *"shoulds"* work. I would buck the system as a way of trying to do things my way (for instance, by not signing up for a degree program) while at the same time doing a version of what I *"should"* do (attending community college instead).

I stopped and started attending community college two more times in my life and completed an online certification in medical billing—each time after doing something rebellious, or experiencing a change, or derailing in my life and feeling that damned sense of obligation to *"get back on track"* and do what I *"should"* be doing.

I had my first job when I was fifteen years old, and to date, my work experience is all over the map. During high school and while attending community college, I worked in a movie theater as an usher/snack bar attendant, receptionist at a hair salon and then in an accounting firm, cashier at a car wash, and a receptionist at a large corporate law firm.

Career-type jobs I have had include: legal secretary, paralegal assistant, claims investigator, insurance adjuster, background investigator, and elementary school aide. There were aspects of each job that I enjoyed but none of them ever felt like my forever thing.

All these jobs and careers had safety in common, or what I had been taught and conditioned to believe was safety: a regular paycheck, benefits, paid vacation and time off, blah, blah, blah. But none of these jobs felt safe to me; they felt chronically and debilitatingly boring and as *"cookie-cutter"* as fuck. I longed for something completely different, and lived with an undercurrent of dissatisfaction as I was always searching for something fun, exciting, and completely my own. It was like it was out there but I just couldn't see or grasp it. My incessant pursuit of safety and stability was showing up in my life as settling, a running-on-a-hamster-wheel feeling of being stuck, along with a growing sense of dread that things were not going to improve. The more I tried to find the fun, joy, and satisfaction in my choices, the more I settled, and the worse my circumstances became, both personally and professionally. My thinking was, *"Well, I've made my bed and now I have to lay in it."* Later on, after telling a friend, their response was, *"No, you just needed to get a new bed."*

I needed to wake the hell up! My wake-up call that jolted me out of bed was the realization that my circumstances were my doing. It was up to me to change them as nobody was coming to rescue me or do it for me. This was the start of the personal development and spiritual journey which led me to the moon.

Enter The Moon

Moonlight drowns out all but the brightest stars.

J.R.R. Tolkien

Or more specifically, the beautiful blue moon of January 2018. The moon represents and is directly tied to our emotions. It reveals to us, if we let it, our inner most emotions, beliefs, stories, hurts, and sorrows as well as our deepest joys, loves, and desires.

We have a blue moon when there are two full moons in a single calendar month. Typically, they happen every few years and one of the ways I work with blue moons is to set intentions that I would like to manifest by the next blue moon. These would normally be longer-term goals. But perfectly and divinely timed for my journey, there was a blue moon in January 2018 followed by a second one in March 2018.

At the January 2018 blue moon, I set an intention to develop an idea or receive an opportunity for a second source of income, not because I needed money, but because I was looking for a side gig that was fun and didn't feel like work or a job. I was looking to satisfy that undercurrent of curiosity, searching, and longing for something different that would be exciting and completely my own. By the March 2018 event, two seemingly unrelated things happened that directly corresponded to my intention. I was introduced to vision boards (fun), and I signed up for an online business course that included a one-to-one coaching session (opportunity to learn how to set up a side gig).

My initial idea was to start some type of consulting business in the same field I was working in because I thought it would be different than having a job. It would be *my own* business. After the coaching call and as I progressed through an associated course, the two seemingly unrelated events merged beautifully together, and the idea of hosting vision board parties and workshops on weekends was born. *Intention manifested.*

Starting the vision board workshops and taking part in the business course birthed the desire to help people transform the dreams on their vision boards into a reality, just like I had. From this, my identity as a manifestation coach was born! The birth of this identity then led me to start an actual business, which I named Blue Moon Manifestations. That unsettled undercurrent of curiosity, searching, and longing for something different that was fun, exciting, and completely my own was starting to settle and surfaced as a flowing river that I am navigating, leading directly to the moon.

At the March 2018 blue moon I created a vision board and set intentions that included building my business and doing some writing on a visible level. By the next blue moon, two years later, I went from recommitting to a journaling practice, to jotting down ideas that I might like to write about, to developing my copywriting and storytelling skills in emails, to my email list, to starting a blog (inconsistently at first but still visible) which were all ways of writing what I wanted to write. And the reconnection to writing has led me to contributing a chapter in this book. *Intention manifested.*

My work with the moon and reconnecting with writing revealed a truth to me about those *"shoulds"* I was talking about earlier. I love words—acronyms and alliteration. I frequently let my mind wander as I doodle with words and letters. I insert symbols, create sigils, put letters in a different order or size, and play around with spelling words differently.

One day I was writing about the *"shoulds"* for one of my weekly live streams. I was writing some notes, doodling, while letting my mind wander. During this process, I wrote the word *"should"* like this: S – h – O – U – L – d and then wrote the sentence, *"The 'shoulds' hold down our soul."* When I looked back at the doodle, I realized that I had written the *"h"* and *"d"* in lower case letters and that the capital letters spelled out the word *"SOUL"* and it seemed the *"h"* and *"d"* stood for *"hold down."* I wrote that little sentence and S – h – O – U – L – d on a sticky note with the comment, *"It's time to ditch the fucking shoulds."* I keep that note posted right by my desk to this day.

From Employee To The CEO Of My Life

I needed a job, but I knew in my gut that getting another *"cookie-cutter"* job could lead me right back down the same road as before. So, I wrote out the type of work I wanted to do, as well as what I wanted it to look and feel like. Then I only applied for jobs that seemed to fit into that criteria or that felt like they may be a possible fit even though what I was being encouraged to do was apply for any *"reasonable"* job. I didn't argue or try to convince others to see things my way, I simply went about applying for jobs I wanted to apply for. It took four months, but I manifested the job that perfectly fit the criteria I established. It was the only job I interviewed for and the pay rate I was offered was higher than what I allowed myself to dream for.

Getting and having that job allowed me to invest in the course and coaching that perfectly led to the birth of my business. And starting a business has been the catalyst for my transformation from identifying and living life as an employee, to identifying and living life as a business owner and the CEO of my life.

Living life identifying as an employee meant working for someone else, doing the work I was assigned to do, saying yes to everything extra that was asked of me because I felt that as an employee, I could not say no without disciplinary action or losing my job. It meant waiting to accrue vacation time that I then had to ask permission to use but instead hoarding it so that I would have it available *"just in case"* something happened, or some kind of emergency came up; it meant feeling like I was trying to cram in and live my life on the weekends.

As I continued to work on myself and get clear on what I wanted, I stepped more and more into living life and identifying as an entrepreneur and boss of my life while still having the role of employee. This transformation has had and continues to have its bumps, detours, uncertainties, doubts, and hard parts.

This shift in perspective and in who I identified as was partially inspired by my boss. During a virtual Q&A, someone asked, *"What can I do to earn more in my job?"* My boss's response was to *"Look at yourself like a business and the company as a customer. Look for ways to make yourself more valuable to the customer (employer) by learning new and diverse skills (aka offerings)."* I took this message and started showing up as an entrepreneur to attract the life I wanted to be living. I freaking love how the Universe works and delivers what we need to hear just when and how we need to hear it.

Intentionally showing up and living life as an entrepreneur in charge of my life while still having the role of employee meant living the life *I intended* to create, regardless of the external circumstances. This meant showing up in my job, in the energy, attitude, and mindset of a manifestation coach. This way, *my focus was on me*, not on the result I wanted.

What did this look like? First, I declared that I was in charge of using and scheduling my time the way I wanted. The Universe delivered. A change in processes in my job allowed me to self-schedule my work appointments instead of having them scheduled for me.

I stated an intention to get rid of all the *"work clothes"* I bought because they were appropriate for my job, clothes which I did not feel great, or *"like myself,"* in. The Universe delivered again: I was allowed to work virtually and I continue to do so. Working from home means I can wear what I like and am comfortable in clothes that make me feel good.

I declared to the Universe that I wanted to shift the balance: I wanted to work less in my job and more on my business. The Universe delivered a workshop on time blocking and batching tasks. Using the skills I learned through the workshop allowed me to work less hours while still getting all my work done. Then the Universe delivered a reduced workload from my job which created more time for growing my business.

As this was unfolding, I realized exactly how much my thinking has changed from the employee identity. I would have immediately started to worry about a reduced workload rather than rejoice in it. For example, I would have fixated on whether I would be able to pay my bills and wondering whether I needed to look for another job would have distracted me, causing me to shift focus. Living life as a business owner, I was thinking things like, *"How the falling away of my job-based tasks was opening up space for something great to come to me through my business."* I saw that *it was up to me* to make up the difference in my paycheck with my business income because I can generate income at any time as an entrepreneur and don't have to wait for payday every two weeks.

Is it a little uncomfortable to shift? Yes, because our brains want to know what is going to happen and when—and that's *ok*. Discomfort is much more desirable than fear and lack thinking.

In the past, realizing this would have sent me into a tailspin, which no longer does. This is truly a *great feeling*. I wouldn't have had the opportunity to see and celebrate how far I have come without experiencing these challenges. I see how transformation results from experiencing and getting through challenges and not simply from the learning. This epiphany also applies to how I show up as a business owner.

I recently told my business coach that I am transitioning from the primarily learning and absorbing information phase into the primarily *implementing* and *taking action phase*. She asked me if I could identify what helped me shift from one way of being into the next and if both learning and doing can exist simultaneously.

After taking some time to reflect on the question, what I shared with her is this: I got my business education through on-the-job training and experience instead of by going to school. My business was a hobby while I allowed my day-job to control my time. I had no previous plans to be an entrepreneur because I was trying to find a way to make the damned established formula work for me; this path was dropped in front of me by the Universe. When that business course was offered in an online community I belong to I thought, *"Why not, it can't hurt."* I stayed true to my intentions.

When I started the course, I didn't have a business idea at all and by the end of the course I started planning vision board workshops on the weekends. About six months into that, I began investing in coaching and additional courses which launched me into what I call the *"I need to learn everything before I really do anything"* season of my business. During this season of learning, implementing and trying, I began developing clarity on what

I want my business to look like. I also realized that being an entrepreneur means I don't have to stick to just one thing—I'm a multi-passionate person and I can carry that into my business.

There's No Going Back

I see my transformation as an ongoing process, like a snake shedding its skin. Once I shed a layer of skin, I will no longer *ever* fit back into the old skin. I may fall back on old habits and old beliefs will creep in, but there is no going back. The fact that my dad and grandparents have done it, as well as many others, shows me that *it is possible for me to do it, too.*

I am the manifestation of my ancestors' dreams so how dare I doubt that I am not capable of not only being successful as an entrepreneur but blowing away any level of success that I currently see is possible. I believe it is all possible and I cannot wait to see how I continue to *Manifest ME!*

Your ancestors outnumber your fears.
Feel their power.

Sarah Tawai

Champions keep playing
until they get it right.

Billie Jean King

Dawn Espinoza

Dawn Espinoza is a multi-published author, visual effects artist, photographer and philanthropist. Her career as an entrepreneur has spanned over thirty years. Dawn's passion is to empower women globally. She is the host of Manifest Bliss and served as a Board Member for both Young Presidents Organization (YPO) and Entrepreneurs Organization (EO). Her two children are her absolute joy! Dawn currently lives in Potomac, Maryland and Miami, Florida.

Soul·Pren·Her The Blueprint For Life, Soul And Business

Dawn Espinoza

Cherish your visions and your dreams
as they are the children of your soul,
the blueprints of your ultimate achievements.

Napoleon Hill

I have always been a curious and creative soul, seeing the beauty in all things. Growing up in Minnesota I was surrounded by nature and its awe-inspiring details. Thinking like an artist has always been part of my DNA.

As I grew older, life was not always beautiful. Our family had its share of challenges. Through my mom's resilience and strength, she taught me how to be tough as nails and to use my voice to go after what I desired. My dad filled me with a love for art and my culture. He is an entrepreneur, and at over eighty years of age, continues to invent and inspire me. Both my parents encouraged me to follow my dreams and helped me to grow my love for making things and my ongoing wonderment with our world. My parents were good at so many things. This fostered in me a desire to be an expert in my field, whatever *"field"* that I chose to be in.

Watching my dad over the years as a creative multi-preneur showed me that I could incorporate everything I was interested in. My lessons came from jobs, school and life experiences.

The Rising Dawn

My journey started in play: dress-up, drawing, and taping shows with my dolls. My friends and I were always in my trunk of wigs and jewelry dressing as Wonder Woman or the Bionic Woman. Lights. Camera. Action. My obsession with magazines and TV evolved when I became a model in my teens. Here I started my love for photography, fashion and beauty. This early time in my life gave me rich experiences that helped foster maturity and discover new parts of myself. I followed new passions and attracted people in my life that have become my teachers and my tribe. I have realized through self-discovery that the tribes we attract are a mirror of who we are at the time and allow our power within to shine.

Being a creative, I have had many passions. I never wanted to be or do just one thing. Many people said to me, *"You can't do it all. Just pick one,"* but *hell no.* I nurtured my desires early on by working hard, weaving all of them into my life.

At eighteen years old, and while most of my friends were off partying at college, I was pulling all-nighters balancing my Estee Lauder inventory control book and managing my own counter. It was a pivotal experience that made me want more, I knew then that I would have my own business.

I could see the big picture, passion married with accountability, discipline and being my own boss. I liked the responsibility and the power that came with it... but I wanted to go further. I pushed away my own limiting beliefs and those around me to pursue what made me feel excited about life. In order to achieve my dreams as both an artist and a beauty industry expert, I left managing the counter and started school.

To put me on this path I attended The College of Visual Arts and then the Aveda Institute. I trained to be at the top of my industry. It was here that I first learned the 80/20 rule, 80% of what you get comes from 20% of what you do. This is a phenomenon that occurs in multiple areas ranging from economics to productivity. In relation to productivity, it says that 20% of the things you do result in 80% of the actions. That means when you prioritize and focus on the correct 20%, 80% of the work will be done. This also makes sense when you think about it in reverse. Most people (myself included at times) tend to cross off the easy stuff first to avoid doing the bulk of the work activities. Then boom! Your day is gone and you have done 80% of your activities, but only 20% of them turned into actions. Prioritization is key to align discipline and fulfillment.

During this time Aveda and their founder Horst also taught me about the ayurvedic lifestyle, a holistic approach to life both within and around us. Throughout my twenties and thirties, this way of living enabled me to more fully enjoy life's experiences.

Just after obtaining my degree, I landed a dream job with Lancôme. I was hired as Spa Manager to open their new Institut de Beaute. I trained at their headquarters in Manhattan, where I was asked to produce live makeovers for them on the *Mall of*

America Show and ABC's *Good Company*. This was my opening into television and film.

By my early twenties, I had created my second dream job and became the Talent Image Coordinator for the ABC affiliate in Minneapolis. They hired freelancers for multiple roles, so I found a loophole and discovered they had no one working with their talent on Mondays. I worked each Monday for free until I convinced them to hire me. Here I took full use of my degrees in cosmetology, massage therapy, makeup artistry, and medical aesthetics. I then sought out mastering wardrobe styling, high-definition makeup, and even set design and lighting techniques.

I continued to connect with others for mentorship and training to develop both facets of my career as an Image Stylist and Clinical Esthetician. I helped found the Minnesota Esthetics Association to offer clinical training on chemical peels and clinical procedures. This enabled me to work for doctors and later partner in a medical spa. My business was growing as I worked day and night to weave all my passions into play. I found myself landing jobs with national television and print clients, working for celebrities and politicians like Prince, President Clinton and the Dole family.

Love, Life And Lessons

As I approached my thirties, I was loving life, living in a high-rise apartment in Minneapolis and driving a pink convertible. Working in television was never dull. I turned down an offer at a film studio in L.A. and began additional work for a national production company. Working for ABC, I had negotiated advanced training into my agreement. They sent me to Washington D.C. for the

CIDESCO Diplomat conference which ended up changing my life as I knew it.

At the conference, I met my *"wasband"* (former husband) and he swept me off my feet. Our long distant romance made me feel an excitement I'd never experienced before. He had enormous drive and energy that fueled me. Soon we were married and I moved to Maryland. We had two children and multiple businesses that paralleled our desires—both individual and supporting of each other's dreams. We were entrepreneurs, starting and not stopping, pursuing whatever we wanted to achieve, from buying our Maryland farm and having that tranquil life for ten years, to property management in destinations that we loved, both in the mountains and by the sea. We traveled, planned, achieved and conquered whatever we set our hearts on.

I was thirty when I had my daughter and almost five years later my son. During this time I partnered with an Oral Maxillofacial Surgeon to open a facial rejuvenation center. I often joke about having two babies at the same time as I worked intently during my pregnancy on creating a unique marriage of wellness and clinical aesthetics. Just after giving birth to my first child, we had our grand opening.

Within a few years, I started to feel the first of many imbalances in my life and well-being. My husband took a position working in San Francisco and Seattle. I began to feel the pressure of so much responsibility on my own. I was caring for our three-year-old daughter with the help of a day school and evening childcare. Working late nights at the center, and being alone on our Maryland farm was challenging. I was blessed with a business partner that honored my desire to cut back on my hours and thankfully within a few months my husband was able to transfer back home.

Once we had our second child I began work for HGTV along with Feld Entertainment and Disney on Ice. I decided that having my own image consulting business would give me more time to enjoy motherhood and life on the farm. It was the perfect fit, allowing me to work early morning hours. Some of my greatest memories are from this time.

By our eleventh year of marriage, however, our relationship began to fall apart. Slowly, chaos replaced my Zen and life was pushing hard all around me. I was having difficulty with clarity in the slow brewing storm. My husband however was thriving, as chaos was his comfort, with more and more mounting in our lives. He returned to school to get his law degree and I found myself feeling alone and questioning what we were doing. He was living in Florida and coming home for long weekends. I desperately wanted to support his dream… yet mine felt lost.

Without my husband, much of the responsibilities fell onto me. It caused me to worry more and I felt my heart breaking. We had what most would call *"it all"* but I was juggling so many balls that by my early forties my nerves were a mess. I began to have panic attacks and health issues that I did not understand. I was far from balanced. I thought that I had Lyme disease, fibromyalgia or that I was allergic to seafood… because I was in denial that it could be panic attacks and stress. It was later that I had to look at how I also thrived on chaos, learning to temper that beast and slay it by choosing less to have more.

Going against the many opinions of others, on our last business together, we fulfilled our dream to be restaurateurs. We developed a large-scale restaurant in Florida complete with an outdoor bar, coffee shop and marketplace. We took it from concept to inception and traveled monthly to see our vision through. It was an amazing experience that I would not trade, but it certainly revealed to me, my limits and fears. Taking control of these made me realize that I was stronger than I imagined.

Singlepreneur

It wasn't long after the whirlwind restaurant years that my marriage ended. I was newly single, and with that, came different challenges. Navigating divorce, juggling my career and family was costly, however, it also taught me some of the most valuable lessons.

I had to develop certain habits—a blueprint, to help me achieve balance, that I could use to be the best version of myself for my family. That meant being present and engaged. I traveled often which was my respite, sparking new joy and recharging my soul. I challenged myself to simplify my life and ask for help where I needed it. Asking for help wasn't easy, I still struggle with it. I enjoyed hosting local events to empower women entrepreneurs to manifest their best life as I tried to do the same.

Designing Her

For nearly a decade I was *Head Gal* of Design-her Gals, a web-based graphic design and stationery company that launched as a unique way to empower women to express and promote themselves as one of the first companies to create a personalized avatar. We had the greatest success growing our online community to over 250,000+

when Oprah added us to her *"Favorite Things"* list and called us *"a ridiculously addictive website."*

My children became teenagers in a blink of an eye. As they have grown, my focus on my business and personal life shifted. My daughter went off to college and has since graduated. My son is in high school, preparing and training in basketball for his college years.

When COVID hit we nested. It was wonderful to have my daughter home and our family together. During this time, I began immersing myself into creating artwork and looked deep within myself and my soul to what felt good. I started feeling my passionate self again.

At the same time the technology (Adobe Flash) which brought *"The Gals"* to life in my design business, was ending. As a result, I made the very difficult decision to close it. Fifteen years is a long time to maintain relevance online, and my team and I made a product we were really proud of. I am the person I am today because of my dedicated team and the founding Gals who continue to inspire me. We all had to figure out how to let go. Saying goodbye to each other and our community was one of the most difficult things I have ever had to do. As a business owner, I felt the weight of responsibility when letting people go. Thankfully, my team made decisions with me every step of the way.

The Soulprenher Blueprint

Life-fulfilling work is never about the money—when you feel true passion for something, you instinctively find ways to nurture it.

Eileen Fisher

It was during this time that I had to re-evaluate what my life and success meant to me. I realized through this introspection, that I wanted to live doing exactly what I love. My life to this point has been a mosaic. Personally and spiritually, I have experienced life's highs and lows, and professionally, a plethora of knowledge in my jobs and soulpreneurship. Both have taught me so many valuable lessons. Through this journey, I have found that my definition of success has changed from wanting shiny things and accumulating financial wealth to living a rich life filled with people, experiences and things I love to do that bring me happiness and joy. I would not have been able to reach this point without developing the blueprint that has kept me on my path to happiness. Practicing just a few of these tools each day helped me through the hardest times and opened me up for greater happiness and success in my life and my relationships.

The following are the fundamental principles of the *Soulprenher Blueprint* that I found to keep me on track:

PRINCIPLE 1:
Map Out Your Dreams
Imagine your future often. Ask yourself, am I fulfilling my soul's purpose, following my passion? What is my legacy? Are your goals in alignment to get you there?

PRINCIPLE 2:
Create A Mindset Mantra
This can be a mission statement, or your *"why."* Repeating it frequently will inspire you to take on its wisdom as truth.

PRINCIPLE 3:

Be In The Game

Putting your financial independence in the forefront sets you up for peace of mind. As a business owner, all my skin is in the game. You must see all angles so you're not blindsided when faced with unforeseen challenges. Death, divorce, COVID-19… shit happens! Bottom-line, be *"In The Game."* Be aware of the game changers, and be ready when the game changes!

PRINCIPLE 4:

Do A Monthly Review

Where are you in business, personal and family life? Recognize the highs and lows. What amount of time is spent in each of these areas? Figure out what you should devote more or less time to and why.

PRINCIPLE 5:

Do MEPS(S) Weekly

Check in with yourself and your tribe: how am I doing: MEPS: Mentally, Emotionally, Physically, Spiritually? Consider adding one more (S) sexually, to help you stay in touch with what brings you pleasure. MEPS is a great practice to add to your meditation or journaling and will give you a daily mindset map.

Quiet your mind.

Rest to de-stress. Relaxation practices like mindfulness meditation, reiki, yoga, or tai chi all improve vital energy. Try visualization—imagining a restful place like the beach or watching a sunset. Consider trying music therapy, color therapy, or chakra balancing. Prayer, journaling, and talking to your tribe or a therapist also help center your soul.

Incorporate Breathing Techniques.

The 4-7-8 breathing method is a quick way to calm the spirit, help you sleep, and relieve anxiety. Start by breathing in for 4 seconds, holding your breath for 7 seconds, and exhaling for 8 seconds. Repeat as needed.

PRINCIPLE 6:

Release Toxic Relationships

We all have them around, emotional vampires that suck your energy. Know when to take a break and how to say no more.

PRINCIPLE 7:

Challenge Your Mind

By learning something new you stimulate your memory. Get creative. Learn a new language, try painting, take a cooking class—mix it up. It doesn't matter if you are *"good at it."*

PRINCIPLE 8:

Practice Soul-preneur-ship

Soul-preneur-ship is the activity of setting up your mind, body and spirit as one. It is taking on the practices of enlightenment in the hopes of achieving your soul's purpose and living a joy-driven life. The soulpreneur knows how to create from a higher dimension and manifest with effortless ease.

PRINCIPLE 9:
Develop Present Moment Awareness (PMA)

It's important to let go, calm down, and get grounded.
We need to listen to ourselves. When one becomes aware that
our present-moment thoughts are not productive, one should
simply let them go. Change a negative thought to a positive one.

Horst Rechelbacher

Practicing your awareness can be done at any given moment—in a meeting, in the shower, or even with your team or family. Do this by noticing all 5 senses and your surroundings. This will bring you back to the here and now and out of your head space.

PRINCIPLE 10:
Your Vibe Attracts Your Tribe

Be around the light bringers, the magic makers,
the world shifters, the game shakers. They challenge you,
break you open, uplift and expand you. They don't let you
play small with your life. These heartbeats are your people.

Danielle Doby

Community building, story-telling through the arts and connecting with people around the world through my travels has always been a core part of my purpose. Your *"Vibe Attracts Your Tribe"* is a mantra that runs deep in my veins. Over time I've come to appreciate and count on *"my tribe,"* the women who support me and inspire me in all aspects of my life. My friendships have spanned the globe. In my life, I have built a community around me of light workers, artisans, goddesses, sistahhhs and badass boss babes. They remind me that we are all on the same wonderfully imperfect journey. With the right tribe, you can lock into your emotional, spiritual and intellectual power to harness a greater collective wisdom. This core community of friendships is the fabric of my life. I have come to understand that cultivating the right tribe holds the keys that will open doors, both within yourself and the world around you. It is up to you to unlock the power and teachings of your tribe. Miracles happen when you can be one with your tribe. That means being vulnerable, and transparent by expressing yourselves from your heart center.

PRINCIPLE 11:
Grace

We often refer to our humanness as our connection to one another. It is the essence of what is kind, tender and compassionate. To be human also means we make mistakes—*"to err is human, to forgive divine."* I urge you to feel into your divinity, the part of you that is the empath and give yourself forgiveness. This is the ultimate form of grace. To hold space for yourself and to just breathe. Grace is essential to move through life in a way that helps us let go. Grace can be a pause, a respite from feeling overwhelmed. It helps us grow by feeling the power in the pause. It helps us with our relationships so we can rise above any pain, sadness, loss, heartbreak or betrayal. Letting go is painful, in all aspects be it closing your baby (business) ending a relationship or saying goodbye to someone or something. In my journey, I have experienced pain in all these areas.

Awakened Path

Dig deeper to connect with your soul's purpose, find your *"why"* and realize your awakened path is not easy. Like adopting any practice it takes work. Our own naysayer—our mind is often the first to get in our way. It robs us of the moment and drags us into our past. We overthink, overshadow, and allow our limiting beliefs to cloud our innermost light. I am guilty of allowing my past experiences and patterns to get in my way. I have completely sabotaged my own progress in the past, missed opportunities and failed at times because of fear and overthinking. I learned that if I don't rise above it, I am held back because of it.

EGO

There is a gift in the ego. It gives you power and drive. Consciousness is the ability to tap into your emotions, subjectively perceive the world around you, and embrace both the light and dark. We exist in both our happy and sad emotions. Ego is not a bad thing. It forms our *Soulprenher Blueprint* of thoughts, feelings and aspirations that we take into action.

SOUL-SELF

Our soul is the truest reflection of our spirit. It is one with the Universe and everything around us. Through my studies, I learned that I could intuitively feel my heart center, my soul-self nudging me to listen to my awareness prior to thought. I achieved this by doing meditations, where I have found both purpose and pleasure.

A New Dawn

My journey has brought me to a *"new Dawn,"* an era where change, challenge, grace and happiness are my new perspectives and focus. I know I have the power to shift my thoughts by letting go of preconceived notions and giving myself grace.

There is an assumption that success is a future goal and it lies ahead of us to unfold. It's easy to get lost in *all the doing* and not enjoy the process if you are always working towards the acquiring. To me, it comes down to happiness. Your soul seeks fulfillment and happiness. If you get quiet and listen, your purpose will be revealed. Mine has.

I believe that stepping back, truly enjoying the process and all the little moments, has led me to discover my purpose. Today, I have given myself the freedom to launch my art and photography businesses on my own time, vision and terms. Creating my art is what brings me joy. My clarity and new perspectives have allowed my new vision and dreams to come to fruition. By tapping into *"The Soulprenher Blueprint,"* I have been able to nurture my budding new businesses because, *"what you give attention to grows."* I am living that life with a commitment to myself—as each moment is *now* to embrace.

She is a warrior capable of slaying the demons in life.
She is a pioneer capable of choosing her own path.
She is a trailblazer capable of achieving new horizons.
Just give her some time and see her bedazzle the world.

Avijeet Das

Anna Gaspari

Anna Gaspari is a published author and soul driven entrepreneur. She became a Spiritual Self Mastery Coach in 2009 and is devoted to teaching women through her coaching and course work about healing money stories and business shame. Anna's passion is to guide her clients towards their new empowered spiritual path. She helps women create a better life by bringing out the best version of themselves. Anna grew up as a hair stylist and has learned to transfer her artistic abilities into her 'course salon.' She has created many programs to help her students achieve their next level.

The Spiritual Grind

Anna Gaspari

*I saw the angel in the marble
and carved until I set him free.*

Michelangelo

You Are The Hero
That You Are Waiting For

No one is coming to save you. Those are the words that I heard that afternoon while having one of my biggest breakdowns. I was hyperventilating in the living room of my dream house, just a few months after moving in. I call it my *"post-house depression."* I would never want to experience that pain again, but it was the catalyst for shaping and preparing me for what was in store for my life.

Standing there, riddled with guilt and self-loathing, so out of control that I was unable to breathe, the words *no one is coming to save you* stopped me dead in my tracks. I remember exactly where I was standing, and I assume the words were from the Holy Spirit.

That moment is still so vivid in my mind. It was as if someone knocked on the door and I stopped crying because I heard something.

Although I know it seems harsh, it was exactly what I needed to hear. Usually, the struggle comes at the time of, or right after, a huge accomplishment, dream, or achievement. For me, it was building my dream home. Actually, getting to design and build a home from scratch on a piece of land was one of the most exciting things I have ever done. More so because it should have never happened. Financially, we should have never been approved for that loan. From the perception of where I was, I thought it was a miracle and knew I was meant to have this house: when something is for you, it cannot be stopped. Then the housing market crashed. I reverted back to my old way of thinking and the circumstances became bigger than my capacity. We immediately went under water. That means that our mortgage was almost as much as our house was worth. We were *"upside down"* as they say. I didn't know then all that I know today about Universal Laws and the energetics of money.

Think of a time when you really wanted something *big*. Something that you had to go *"all in"* on. Something that you had to exchange blood, sweat, and tears for. Now tell me after you said *yes* to the thing, didn't all your limiting beliefs or challenges come up right behind it? Until we learn the lessons—like *for real,* learn the lessons—we are just going to continue struggling. Pain has purpose but struggle is a choice. This is key to understanding: we always have a choice.

You may be thinking, what does any of this have to do with business? For me it had *everything* to do with business. It was through my *"post-house depression"* experience that I found my purpose. The message about my purpose didn't come the way I thought it would. I used to think clarion trumpets would sing and rainbows would show up. Maybe I thought I would be tiptoeing through tulip fields too.

Oh no, no. It came packaged up like a big bag of poo. I mean, up until then, I thought life was just about working, finding a husband, having kids, and living modestly like my parents did. I mean, looking back, I always was a *little extra*, but I easily could've lived a totally different life if the housing market didn't crash.

Chaos To Clarity

What exactly was the solution? More money. At the time, I was a stay-at-home mom of my first two babies, aged four and six. I was a hairdresser, so I was doing a couple of haircuts here and there but not enough to pay bills. My husband was a state trooper. We lived paycheck to paycheck. I had to do something. I knew that it had to be me which is why that day in my living room changed everything for us.

Chaos leads to great opportunities. Sometimes opportunities find you but other times, you must seek them out. It is part of the game that God plays with us. Champions are not built on the field on game day. They are built in practice when no one is watching. They are built when recovering from an injury. When knocked down, athletes get up and get back at it. I had my couple of months of deep depression and by the grace of God, I listened to that small still voice that told me to go to the computer and search the phrase, *"work from home."*

From that search, I found the occupation, *"life coach."* After more internet searches, I found a woman who was tapping on her face and body to create more money in her life. I was desperate so I gave it a whirl. I listened to that video and was fascinated. *"Well shit,"* I thought. *"I can tap my face for more money."* So I tried it. I liked it. I started to feel different. I was in a world of personal development and didn't even know it. All I knew was that I was lost in the magic of finding out that I could have more than I had *if* I changed my thinking. I suspended the disbeliefs one by one. I started to believe that I could do anything. I kept with the healing modalities that were being introduced in my life and was willing to learn a totally different skill and new knowledge.

I looked deeper into life coaching and then found Spiritual Life Coaching. The circuits lit up. The bells went off and I knew *I had to* become this. From that moment, in my living room to me making a decision to go to school, was about six months. In the meantime, I had my third baby and by 2009, which was two years later, my life took a total 180-degree turn.

I received my coaching certification, started as a sales rep in an MLM (Multi-Level Marketing) company and flew to the top ranks of that company within a short period of time. I went from making no money to six figures. It was all me. I made a commitment and decided to raise my standards. It worked. I was the hero I was looking for.

Everything Happens For A Reason

The best thing we can do for ourselves in life is fix our shit, or as I like to say, *"transcend your bullshit."* Things get so much better after taking responsibility for the choices we have made in life. Blaming anyone or anything else is exhausting. Finding the hidden gems, lessons, and storylines have become adventurous and freeing for me. And to be honest, in order to get to your *next level,* you don't even need to heal anything specific from your past, *yet.* You just need to decide if life is better than what you currently are living and what you are willing to exchange for it.

From time to time, I may see an old pattern reappear. Maybe I notice I'm feeling sorry for or trash-talking myself. I have to pivot and correct as soon as I am aware. I say it out loud, *"Cancel, Cancel."* Yes, I do. I call out my own shit often. If I buy my own BS I will keep buying others. People don't pay me to make excuses for them, they pay me for results. In order to get results, it takes disciplining the mind and being radically honest.

The moral of what I am saying here, is that you are reading this because your eyes are meant to, whether you know it or not. Gravity still works even if we aren't consciously aware of it, right? Same way with the Universal Laws.

Being aware of the *dragon voice* in you, is *key* to knowing her dirty little tricks. You can override her at any time. Everything you do is a conscious or unconscious decision. Time to rise up, friend. Everything happens for a reason.

Cliff Notes:
How To Get What You Want Quickest

Who doesn't love Cliff Notes? I know I do. Now this doesn't mean that you don't have to go through the lessons. You must integrate knowledge, or you will live a delusional life. Ready? I am going to give you the fastest route that I personally have found to manifest the things I've wanted. You've heard the saying, change your thoughts, change your life? Well, I agree, but change your thoughts about what?

- Change your thoughts around who you think you are and change your life.

- It's who you think you are that is holding you back.

- Your self-identity is everything: not who the world thinks you are or who you were told you are—it is who *you* think you are.

Let me give you my own real-life example: I grew up in a hairstylist's paradigm. My late father, Luigi, was a barber. He immigrated here from Italy. My mother's sister, Mia, also came here to America from Italy and became a hairdresser, as did my godfather, Uncle Frank. It's a family thing.

My dad purchased and operated his own barbershop in Metuchen, NJ., for many years. It was called "Luigi's Styling Shop." Straight out of high school, I became a licensed cosmetologist. On a sunny afternoon while my dad and I were in my living room he said, *"If you want to go to college, you are going to have to pay for it. Instead of college, you are going to come work for me at the shop. You will make a lot of money."*

That's about all I heard and remembered, but what I *subconsciously decided* was a different story. That day, knowing my friends all planned to go off to college, I decided that I *"wasn't worthy"* of being educated. I decided that day that I would work like my dad and depending on how hard I worked would determine how much money I would make. The more people I worked on meant more money. That's a lot of hours. I decided I wasn't worthy of being *"smart."* I decided because I was good at something, it meant that I had to do only that to get paid. I internalized that I didn't have *"permission"* to do or have what I wanted.

I'm so grateful I had the honor to work beside my dad for eight years. I don't regret one second of it; it happened exactly as it was meant to.

Everything happens for a reason.

A Stallion In A Barn

I felt like a wild animal in a barn, like a stallion, kicking and bucking to get out. Not using my voice led to bad relationships and massive emotional contortions to avoid confrontation. I always wondered what was out there that I missed, because the decision to work at my father's barbershop wasn't mine. All those years I was not using my voice to make decisions because I didn't know any better. I was doing what I was taught and expected to do. Eight years. Now that I can look back, I can see how blessed I was and the powerful lessons that time gave me.

And after coaching thousands of women, one thing that I have recognized is that most women feel pent up in some way. Most women have something, and they wonder, *what if I had done that instead*, not in a regretful way, but in a curious manner. If it holds a strong sense of purpose, it can be devastating.

Do you remember a time when you felt held back by someone or something? Maybe you can journal about the lessons that has taught you. I know that I am a much better teacher and coach due to my past experiences. No matter what stage of life I have been in, I didn't always have to *heal* in order to make any decisions that moved my life forward. Healing is a journey that continues to blossom.

The mere imagination and allowing the thought to become possible is enough to start to open doors. I had experiences and felt worthy enough over time by learning new skills and meeting new people in my life. I eventually gained the courage to tell my dad that I wanted to explore working in bigger salons closer to home. Breaking his vision (heart) of me taking over his barbershop was one of the toughest things I ever had to do. How many times do we hold back to make someone else feel adequate? My teacher used to advise us against, *"peace at any price."* I gave up a lot of my own peace to make others happy.

Peace is my most valuable asset. It is what we all seek in the end. Personally, I gained more of my father's respect because people admire courage. They admire a person with a vision and a dream to move in a different direction, even if it's not what they expected. If you can channel your *"stallion in a barn"* energy into something, what would that *"something"* be?

Being Bold

Telling someone what you want can be scary sometimes, but it's the courage that takes you to that whole other level. I changed my identity and saw myself differently. Upgraded. There are times in your workspace when we get complacent. The money is no longer enough to keep us somewhere because humans are born to expand and grow personally and professionally.

Professionally. That's the word. Going *pro.* There comes a time in your business when you know you need to go *pro.* If growth and professionalism had a baby, its name would be PRO. It takes great *boldness* to enroll in a level of leadership.

When I was twenty-six, and starting phase two of my career, I had time on my hands. At least I thought I did. I am not putting a number or phase to where I am now, but no matter how old you are, there is no more time to waste. I would tell my twenty-six-year-old self that too. The idea of time can be a thief. My dreams, your dreams, they are happening right now. You may not be experiencing that reality presently, but, the identity it takes to live that out is available to you always. Be bold and go after the things you want for your life and business. *Now.*

Slay The Dragon

I believe we have two voices: The one you're listening to is your Master. There is the Ego Mind. I call my Ego Mind, *Dragon Girl.* Finally, there's the Miracle Mind. That is the higher mind. Both the Ego Mind and the Miracle Mind are vying to get our attention.

One of the questions I will ask you is, what would you trade your life for? What would you give your blood, sweat, and tears for?

Going back to the day that I had that shift in my living room of my dream home, I decided to listen to my Miracle Mind that day. I didn't know exactly how I was going to afford to stay in my house, but I did know one thing: God did not bring me this far to take it away from me. So, I listened to the voice that said, *"work from home."*

At that time, I had a Dell laptop with tons of viruses in it— I needed a lot of patience just to look things up. I went on the search for *"how to make money from home."* My seeking led me to where I am today. That was sixteen years ago. So, if you feel that you are seeking something, or maybe even a little lost, just remember this: what you are looking for, is looking for you too. My best advice here is to suspend any belief even for a moment that life doesn't get better than this. Because it *absolutely does.* You don't need to prove anything to anyone at this moment. You don't need to heal any past traumas right now. You just need to *believe* that there is something greater than you conspiring to bring peace and prosperity into your life. Which voice is mastering you? Use your *Dragon Girl* voice to slay, one decision at a time.

Business And Healing

I found my personal storyline through business. I know that my business helped me heal. I know that I continue to heal through building my business. I exchange my blood, sweat, and tears for exactly what I'm doing right now. Nothing lights me on fire more than knowing I am helping other women like myself conquer their fears, transcend their limiting beliefs, return to a path that is a spiritual one, and fulfill their life's purpose.

I know that inspiring others is what I am here to do. I do that by speaking my own truth, by expressing who I am through what I do, and manifesting the life that I desire. When I do these things I give permission to other women to do the same. I do this for the women that may not have believed in themselves enough. I create containers and space for them in one way or another so that my energy, and my existence can make a difference to her. People will know it's possible when they can see it in you. If they can see it in you, they can see it in themselves.

When things get really hard, do you just quit? What are the things in your life that you just won't quit on? I know writing a book was a dream of mine. And when this opportunity came up again, I knew it was time for me to say yes.

Your time won't always have the right circumstances attached. God doesn't check your bank account to see if you can afford what you want. He calls you out to the waters where you must exercise your faith. The *how comes after the commitment.* I knew I just had to say yes and what tagged along behind my commitment was a *"nasty dragon girl."* She reminded me of all of my failures, of all of my fear-based identities, and that *nasty dragon girl* got me behaving in a way that didn't serve me.

Once you learn how your lower self operates, you can then override it. You can override anything. That's why so many people miss opportunities way too often. But if it's meant for you, it will come back around in your life. And that's why I know that any book opportunity I had in the past is being played out right now for me.

Did I feel like I had the skills to write a book? No, of course not. But I said yes anyway. This was an amazing chance for me to start. And I am the queen of starting things. I will say, I don't always finish the things I start, but when I do, it's usually pretty amazing.

Be Willing To Be Misunderstood

When I started on my life coaching journey, I honestly did not know what I was doing, and how I was going to do it. I was just following the *pull.* Did you ever feel a force that just pulls you and you cannot logically understand what it is?

In 2006, when this *pull* happened to me, my friends and family would say, *"you're doing what?"* Nobody understood me. *You must be willing to be misunderstood.* And something really funny happened. After a little while, I noticed that when I kept the promises to myself that I spoke about, people stopped questioning me as much. My inner voice said, *"Just watch me."* You kind of have to blow your own mind from time to time.

Something else funny happens along the way when things go really well—you forget what you did to get there. Maybe it's not that you forget, maybe it is that unconsciously somewhere along that storyline you tell yourself that it can't be that good any longer and you need to over complicate things. Or maybe it's just that life happens and then we look at how we can self-sabotage ourselves. Or maybe it's a little bit of everything. We are programmed to self-destruct.

Override that bitch.

I get to determine how I want to see things. You get to determine how you want to see things. We create the interpretation and meaning for everything in our journey. So, when I *understand* why I created the meaning for whatever has happened, I can change the narrative. This is what I call the Miracle Mind Shift.

Whatever you believe is true. The Universe has a *yes* energy to it and it wants to give you everything that you believe. Not everything that you want. This is where we have to work on our spiritual mindset and faith in a greater God than man. If you believe that you can, the Universe will conspire to make that happen. If you believe that you can't, the Universe will conspire to make that happen too.

Welcome to *The Spiritual Grind*™!

Business For Good

We get to use our business for good. When I made the shift away from focusing on the money, I gained a lot more peace and clarity. Even though I'm a money coach—and of course there is nothing wrong with focusing on money from time to time—the ride is so much sweeter when we *focus on who we are serving*. Be in the world, but not to be *of it*. I am playing *in it*. The worldly things are fun, beautiful, exciting, and miraculous. But none of it defines who we are and where we are going.

Integrate

I may be inspiring you and shifting something within you. But still, that will never be enough for you to actually live your dreams. You are going to have to make a decision *right now.*

What is your next *yes* step? Remember what I had said earlier? *The commitment always comes before the how.*

Whatever it is that you imagine, there are people who are waiting for you to do that. Just like this book. I could've used a lot of excuses, then thought: why *not* me. I imagined the girl with her cup of tea, cuddled up in her pajamas in her favorite spot reading this. I imagined her hanging on to every word with hopes that my next thing that I would say would be the thing that she needed to hear in order to believe deeper in her own dreams again. When my focus turned to that, I got lost in my own story. Don't you want to get lost in your own story? Don't you want the movie to end and have people leave the theater feeling so great knowing that life is so good? Don't you want the people in your life that you're building a life for to be inspired by your gifts?

We see not from our eyes yet, but from our hearts. Today is the best day of the rest of your life. Today you have a blank slate, you have a pen, you have a chisel: you get to carve her out just as you imagined her. Make it happen because this is it. Life is now. Do it messy. Do it hard. Do it loud. Whatever way you feel called to do it, just do *the thing*. The world needs you to become her. Your people are waiting.

Never underestimate the power of dreams
and the influence of the human spirit.
We are all the same in this notion.
The potential for greatness lives within each of us.

Wilma Rudolph

A strong woman looks a challenge
in the eye and gives it a wink.

Gina Carey

Jamie Gates

Jamie Gates is a published author and the Founder/CEO of Badass Boss Babe Club and Little Hot Pink Book. Her mission is to help women live a life full of joy and abundance. She is committed to creating a collaborative community along with mentorship and coaching for women to feel supported, uplifted and empowered to transform their mindset, business, and body so that they can be a Badass Boss Babe and thrive in all areas of life.

Becoming A Badass Boss Babe

Jamie Gates

*You will recognize your own path when you come upon it,
because you will suddenly have all the energy
and imagination you will ever need.*

Jerry Gillies

The Lemonade Stand

As far back as I can remember, I always wanted to be an entrepreneur. It all started with my first lemonade stand, a common entry to entrepreneurship for kids in North America. Mine gave me a sense of pride. I had seen others doing the stand and now I had one of my own. I was so happy that people were coming to my booth and I asked my dad to build a permanent structure at the end of our driveway so that customers could come by and order their lemonade. Well, *that* idea didn't fly. It was the 1970s, no one saw that I was a trailblazer at age eight—now we see coffee drive-thrus everywhere. I didn't drink coffee back then, but the idea was the same.

I dreamed about throwing parties for people, then later became a wedding planner and launched a corporate event planning business. It was fun, but it wasn't fulfilling for me. I went back to the corporate world and worked for an internationally known company where I threw parties for my clients and didn't have to deal with the headaches of running my own business by myself. However, I felt like something was missing. I still had this longing to be an entrepreneur, but I was struggling with what that looked like for me. I couldn't figure out how to turn my lemons into lemonade.

My Two Cents

To meet new people when I moved to Atlanta, Georgia, I started a networking group. When life called me back home to Alaska, I decided to begin a networking chapter there too. Then a series of events led me to Los Angeles, California, so I founded my third chapter. I saw my networking groups as a hobby. I charged people just enough to cover the costs of running the events.

Within these groups, women began to seek my guidance on business: I showed them how they should introduce, present, and brand themselves. To help the group, I decided to start giving presentations during the events on marketing tips and how to build a network. The women in the group told me that I should start charging for my services. I thought, *"What?! Crazy thoughts! Why would someone pay for me for my thoughts, for my two cents?"*

After months of hearing that I should charge for my advice, I finally agreed. Overnight, I created a brand, a website, and did a competitive analysis and research on services and pricing. By the next networking meeting I had created my *"little business"* and nervously presented it to the group of women. They loved it. Immediately, I got *two paying clients.*

Over the years my networking group and my coaching/consulting businesses have merged, evolved, and grown. I've added new offerings and ditched services that cost me time, money, or my sanity. And I learned that people were willing to pay for my *"two cents!"*

Sometimes people go searching for their purpose in life. My purpose kept hunting me down. Once I realized that what I was doing for a living is me *living out my purpose and passion,* I felt guided and grounded. It hasn't always been easy, but I can tell you from my heart: it has been worth it helping so many women create and launch their businesses and grow both personally and professionally. Like lemonade, some of my journey has been sweet, and some of it tart. I've learned some lessons the hard way.

Surround Yourself Well

Surround yourself with people
whose eyes light up when they see you coming.

André De Shields

One of the most difficult parts of starting out as a solo entrepreneur is going at it alone. There were many times in my journey where I felt like giving up. Had it not been for the women I chose to surround myself with, I probably would have. We all need to feel encouraged, believed in, and seen.

After dealing with some major health issues, I had decided to do a detox. Unbeknownst to me, this would lead to a detox in multiple areas of my life. Not only did I eliminate foods that didn't nourish my body, I got rid of things in my life that were not healthy for me, my soul, and my overall well-being. I detoxed my environment, my social media, my TV shows, and people.

The hardest detox was the people. Friendships dissolved; this was heartbreaking. But in the end, I realized many, but not all, of the relationships that went away were for the best. As a people pleaser, I had been surrounding myself with women who drained me and sucked the life out of me. I realized that I was making changes in my business to suit *their* needs instead of staying true to the vision I had for my mini empire. My brand had evolved into something that barely resembled me. Over the years, the color purple came to represent my brand, yet it's not one of my favorite colors. But my *"board members"*—those women I let into my inner circle of my life—swayed me into doing what *they* wanted and I drifted away from being authentically me. I was playing small and holding back.

The problem with people pleasing is that it's like a sugar habit you can't quit. You indulge a little, it doesn't satisfy you, but you keep going back for more and the cycle repeats. I realized there were people in my life that were making me feel this way. What did I do? I started distancing myself from them. You don't need to eliminate people completely from your life, just pay attention to the five people you spend the most time with. How do they make you feel?

As you raise your vibration, some people will leave. Just like when you take two magnets that are stuck together and turn them around, they will repel each other. That doesn't mean the magnets, or the people, are bad. They just aren't meant to stick together anymore.

There were also a few people that the Universe decided to remove for me. And, damn, were these hard lessons for me to learn. Because there were areas of my life that were not yet healed, I kept attracting the same type of people. These people were not nourishing my soul and making me feel fed. Much the opposite. I would leave their presence only to feel drained, disappointed, or full of self-doubt. But it wasn't obvious at first. If I met someone and they made me feel bad right away, of course, I wouldn't want to be around them again. These were people who externally seemed great, but after a while they would start saying things like, *"Are you sure you're capable of doing that?"* After a while, I started talking to myself the same way they talked to me and I developed major doubts about being an entrepreneur. I mean, who the heck did I think I was, thinking that people would pay me for whatever I think I can do? Serious self-doubt crept in.

Thanks to my emotional detox and the Universe stepping in to weed out those who were not good for me, I learned a valuable lesson: choose your friendships and business partners wisely. Also, keep your friends close and your *frenemies* far, far away. Today, my people—my tribe, my flock—are women who are filled with love, joy, and laughter. I have a group of women who lift me up, and another group I can be raw and vulnerable with as they help me replenish what I have given away. I am creating the tribe I had always wished I was a part of.

Remember that not every person who comes into your life is meant to stay there. And not everyone who stays, needs to fill all the roles. That's why we surround ourselves with a whole community that fills different needs for us. It's how we get nourished so we can continue to give and be of service. Surround yourself with women who support, uplift, and empower you to be the most fabulous version of yourself. Surround yourself with women who have leveled up, so they inspire you to achieve more. And you can also surround yourself with women who need you to inspire them. It is in the giving that we receive.

Set Your Soul On Fire

Shortly after I rebranded, my boyfriend and I took a road trip from Los Angeles to the Midwest to visit his family for Christmas. While we were making our way across the country his six-year-old niece texted him and asked what our favorite animals were. Um... my favorite animal? I realized at that moment I didn't really *have* one. So, I thought, *"What would be a fun answer for a little girl..."* and blurted out, *"The flamingo."* On Christmas day, she excitedly handed me the gift she made for me: a beautiful painting of a flamingo! It was a hot pink flamingo, with a black background, and sparkling stars all over it. It matched my brand *perfectly*, and thus, SUE, our mascot was born. I never thought that my company would have a mascot.

My research revealed that the word flamingo is derived from the Spanish word flamenco which means fire and it is also a style of dance. To me, it means, find *that thing* that fills your soul with fire and passion, so much so, that it makes you dance with excitement.

Let That Joy Out!

Over the years of working with many women who want to be entrepreneurs, I have heard many say a version of, *"Yes, Jamie, I want that joy but I have no idea what is my purpose or my passion."* *"My life is dull…"* *"I can't even imagine something igniting a little spark much less a raging fire in my soul that I can't contain."*

Here are some tips that I have used to help others find their joy and their passion:

TIP 1:

Start where you are with what you have. You already have your joy and passion inside you. We just might need to *dig deep* to find it. But it's there, Babe.

TIP 2:

Remember that sometimes people go searching for their purpose and other times it finds you.

TIP 3:

Pay attention to the signs around you, the common threads that have weaved in and out of your life. It might be deep, but it's there.

A *free flow* of your thoughts and brain download is an excellent exercise to begin. Ask yourself these questions and write down everything and anything that comes to mind.

- When I was a child, what did I want to be when I grew up?

- What were some of the big ideas I've had?

- What do I love doing?

- What brings me joy?

- What makes me really angry? (Many businesses were created to solve a problem or create a solution because someone was upset about the way things were!)

- What do people repeatedly tell me I do well?

- What's my superpower?

- What are my unique talents?

- If money were not an issue, what would I spend my days doing?

- When I think back on the happiest moments in my life, what was I doing?

Is there a pattern? Even if it's just a small handful of items that are related, what do you see? Maybe *that thing* that you've discovered, that little fire in your soul, isn't something you can turn into a business. *You still need to do it.* Passion fuels our purpose and fills our lives with joy in the midst of our storms and struggles. Whatever you do, *do it like you mean it.*

I Can Do It Better Myself

As solopreneurs, we tend to do *everything* ourselves. Sure, you can, but if you continue to try to *do it all* you will burn yourself out. How do I know this? That was *me* for a long time. My head was filled with thoughts like, *"It will take way too long to teach someone else how to do what I can do." "There's no way in hell I'm giving someone else control of any part of my business." "Sure, I'd love to delegate but where do I even start."*

Here is where you start:

1. Make a list of everything you do in your business. Take a week or two with a notepad by your side, an excel spreadsheet or an online project management program like Asana or Notion and track everything you do. And I mean E-V-E-R-Y-T-H-I-N-G. It may seem like an overwhelming task but believe me, it will help you in the long run and save you time down the road.

2. Now you have a list with tasks and time spent on each one. Review, sort, and categorize each task. I recommend you do this at the end of the two weeks so you can view everything together and group tasks that are similar. Notice the patterns. This is also a good time to pay attention to when you are your most productive and creative self so you can plan your days for maximum results.

3. Look at your tasks that absolutely need to be done and consider which do not absolutely need to be done by *you*. Now imagine six months from now you have consistently been delegating these tasks to someone else and you have more time to focus on your money-making activities to grow your

business! If you are always working on running it, you will hit a ceiling and limit the growth you can achieve.

4. Focus on your area of genius, those things you can do in your sleep while other people struggle to do them, and find people who can do the other tasks for you. Start small so you can scale big. And remember to surround yourself well.

Bring Out The Bubbles

The more you celebrate in life, the more life will give you to celebrate. Being a *badass* is all about *mindset*. It is about being relentless in the pursuit of your dreams. It takes grit, a daily dose of gratitude and determination.

When you wake up every day, start it with gratitude. A gratitude journal is a great way to have clarity and begin your day with a positive mindset. Keep the journal by your bedside and make a list of ten things you are grateful for, and one person you need to forgive. The exercise of forgiveness is not for them, it's for you. *That one person may even be you.*

There's probably a lot of shit you've done in your life that you regret or would change. Lean into it, deal with it, and give yourself some grace. Erase that looped soundtrack playing in the back of your head and fill it with gratitude. *What you think about, you bring about.* When we change our state of being from one of worry to gratitude, big changes happen quicker. Start believing in good things.

Then bring out the bubbles to celebrate. Find ways to incorporate the feeling of having a bubbly life. Imagine if every day you were walking around feeling effervescent and full of joy. Indulge in self-care, perhaps a *bubble bath*, have some quiet, alone time, and focus on all the things you are grateful for.

You can also have an evening gratitude ritual with a glass of bubbles. An idea is to choose your favorite *sparkling something*, whether it be water or another beverage. Pour yourself a glass, unwind, and make a list of everything that happened in your day that you are grateful for. Celebrate your successes: raise your glass and cheer your accomplishments big and small. I got a new client! Cheers! I completed that big project! Cheers! I started a project! Cheers! I cleaned my desk! Cheers!

This is not about the drinking. It is about *the action of recognizing and acknowledging what you have achieved*. Big goals and dreams are often achieved by a series of many, many small steps.

Girl, You've Got This

One of the things I really enjoy doing is going on road trips. So for my fiftieth birthday, my boyfriend and I drove to Boise, Idaho from Los Angeles to celebrate with my daughter, who went to college there. Los Angeles was still on lockdown because of the pandemic, so we loved the idea of actually being able to go out on the town to celebrate, the three of us, especially for this milestone birthday. I had been to Boise many times and loved it there; Jeff was excited to explore a new city with me.

On our way back to L.A., we made the decision to move to Boise. We didn't give ourselves much of a timeline to do this either.

We started preparing and packing everything, having garage sales, and hiring movers, so we could move *in less than one month*. What the *flamingos* were we thinking? I was a bit beyond stressed and I posted on Facebook:

"Have you ever had one of those moments in your life where you're just wishing/praying/hoping someone just runs up alongside you, grabs your hand says "It's all good! You've got this!"

The outpouring of support was amazing. It helped get me through the rest of it. But what truly blew me away was the next day at our moving sale, a stranger looked at me and out of nowhere said *"You've got this."*

Sometimes we feel like we are alone and going at it all by ourselves and in reality, there are people who would love to support, uplift, and empower you. We may need to ask for help, for the support or just put it out into the Universe that you need someone to run up alongside you, grab your hand and tell you, *"It's all good, you've got this!"*

Being A Badass Boss Babe

I'm often asked about my company name: Badass Boss Babe Club. Each word has an intention behind it. It really is about the mind, body, and soul connection. I mentioned that *Badass* is about your mindset. It's about grit, grace, and gratitude. *Boss* is about being the CEO of your business and your life. *Babe* is about making healthy choices and practicing self-care to feel good about yourself inside and out.

BADASS

Don't be afraid to take some risks. Do the things that frighten you. I didn't think that I had a safety net, but I did. It was *me*. Like Glinda told Dorothy in the *Wizard of Oz*, I've always had the magic inside me, I just had to discover it for myself. I learned that I had within me everything I needed to be successful. The same is true for you. When you show up, the Universe conspires on your behalf.

BOSS

The best CEOs know what is happening in their company. They can see the big picture and dive into the details or dig deep when needed in order to change course. To be the CEO of your life and your business… *pay attention.*

Pay Attention To:

- Who you are spending most of your time with. Are their words or actions helping you be the most radiant version of you?

- How your body feels.

- Your business and your bank account.

- Your customers and what they are saying. If it's bad, figure out why and get your shit together or get rid of those customers if they are just drama.

- Your thoughts and your doubts. What is your self-worth and what is affecting it?

- Your past and what keeps creeping up on you and deal with it, with grit, grace, and gratitude.

BABE

Find your balance. What does that mean? Do a balance of things that *flocking* scare the shit out of you as well as the things that you can do in your sleep. Take action every day to be a Badass Boss Babe. Sometimes that even means taking a break. Rest and recharge are actions too.

CLUB

It's worth repeating to surround yourself well. Spend time with your flock, your tribe. There are so many amazing communities for women to connect and collaborate. If you can't find one that works for you, create your own, like I did.

Walk like A Flamingo

I found that my beautiful hot pink flamingo is the embodiment of who I am, what I believe in and live by. I named her SUE as an acronym for: *Support, Uplift, and Empower.* My personal mission is to support, uplift and empower women so that they can thrive in life and business.

Flamingos are also transformative in nature. They aren't born pink. They nourish and grow into their *pinkness*, like I did. Flamingo personalities are often characterized as being open minded, vivacious, and heart-centered.

I came up with my own mantras of what the flamingo means to me and my life.

- Stand tall and stand out.
- Be bold.

- Spend time with your flock.

- Be flexible.

- Wade into life.

- Don't be afraid to get your feet wet.

- Set your soul on fire.

- Seek a balance in your life.

- Feed your mind, body and soul.

- Don't be afraid to ruffle a few feathers.

Everything you need is already within you. You are an amazing, unique creation with talents and skills that no one else can offer the world. The world needs you to stand tall and stand out, be bold and say it louder for those in the back. And remember to set your soul on fire so that you can shine bright to light the way for others. The journey to finding yourself is filled with obstacles, questions, chaos and lemons. It is what you do with it that makes the difference.

If life gives you lemons, don't settle for simply making lemonade.
Make a glorious scene at a lemonade stand.

Elizabeth Gilbert

Christine Henderson

Christine Henderson is a published author and President/Founding Officer of Henderson Automotive Inc., which serves the Durham Region, in Ontario, Canada, since 1998. Christine's business experience spans over twenty-five years. As a female owner of an automotive service and repair facility, she has pushed through many obstacles, industry bias and social norms to achieve success. Christine has been featured in, and written for, automotive trade magazines and has made numerous appearances on her local TV and radio stations. She is passionate about making each and every day enjoyable in both her business and family life.

Steel-Toe Dreams

Christine Henderson

You've always had the power.
You just had to learn it for yourself.

Glinda the Good Witch
The Wizard of Oz

We met at the restaurant where I worked. He was funny, charming, and very attentive. For a girl who had been raised in a very jagged family, with a lack of self-esteem and self-worth, the attention he offered was exciting. Braeden's family were very accepting, and I fell in love with them too. We bought our first house together, and then he purchased a small business that he ran. My life was good and I was happy. From where I had come from, this was a dream come true.

I can't remember the exact moment that this idea of opening an automotive garage was sprung on me to run by myself, but I do remember thinking, *"How hard could it be?"* I had been told that there was a lot of money in automotive repair, and all we had to do was hire a *"guy or two."* I'd be stupid *not* to—at least according to my husband.

A prime location automotive shop had become vacant with a lot of parking, a ton of traffic, and reasonably priced. *Yep, easy,* young naive me thought. All I had to do was answer phones, write a check or two, and collect the money. We hired a technician, and opened the doors in November 1998.

The first two years that I ran the shop were a total learning curve. There was a lot to know just for ordering parts and scheduling. The only thing I knew about cars was how to fill them with gas, to call someone when the check oil light came on, and that if my car required too many trips to a mechanic, I could buy a new one. So in my new business, I started a routine of self-education. Each time a customer asked a question, out of necessity, I would say, *"I'm sorry, but I'm not sure. Let me go find out for you."* I would go talk to the technician to get an explanation, and go back to the client and repeat it. This educated me *and* the customer. I also spent time in the shop watching the techs work, and asking every question I could think of. As time passed, I was able to answer more and more questions without consulting the technician. We bought some new equipment, and hired a second technician. Things were going well.

In 2000, Braeden sold his business. We decided that he would come take over at the shop, and that I would reduce my hours and go part-time (paperwork and banking only) and that we would start a family. Our daughter was born in 2001 and I stopped working at the shop altogether to be home with her.

Dreams Turn To Nightmares

With the pressures of a small business, things at home had started to become more challenging. There were so many red flags that indicated the financial mess that would come. While our debt load grew, Braeden made secret frivolous purchases. He would leave the garage in the middle of the day to buy *"expensive toys"* and ignored the needs of the clientele. When I couldn't pay the bills, Braeden told me it was because the staff weren't performing—but I wasn't allowed to speak up and reprimand them. In hindsight, I should have taken action when I first noticed Braeden's unfounded accusations and the large amounts of money disappearing, but I didn't. In any small business, efforts (and a sprinkle of luck) generally equal results. Because the effort dwindled, so did the results. Our personal and business finances soon became a hot mess.

In 2003, Braeden was offered a high paying contract position through a longtime friend, and he wanted to pursue it. I didn't want to close the business, so we decided that I would go back to work at the garage until his contract ended. Kendall, our daughter, who was fourteen months at that time, went to a family member for daycare, so I could work full-time.

The first couple of weeks in the shop were a challenge for me. I believed in what we were doing, and that this was the best decision to help repair our finances. Secrets that Braeden had been keeping started to come to light. Accounts that were past due, purchases that I didn't know about, and oh yes, there was hidden money. When confronted, Braeden always had a reason and an excuse about what happened; that it was my fault, or a customer's fault, or a supplier's fault. My favorite of his excuses was, *"I figured you knew about that.*" I agreed with everything he said, and I spent the next three months making deals with creditors, paying down as much debt as possible, and consolidating the rest any way I could.

As a mom, I felt like I was missing out on some great moments of my daughter's life, so I would come home at night and devote my evenings to taking her to the park, playing outside, or just spending time cuddling with her. After six months, just when we seemed to have a decent routine, his contract ended.

Braeden decided he wanted to go back to the shop, as we had planned; but after the first time, I had serious reservations. I first suggested that he find employment elsewhere, then I suggested that we work in the shop together. He made it clear that if I was still going to work, he wouldn't be. I decided to continue working at the shop, and left Kendall at home with him. It felt like this was the beginning of the end. Our home became a hostile environment.

While my marriage deteriorated, things at the business were getting bigger and better. More clientele, more work, and more lessons daily of how the industry and self-employment worked. I started going to after-hours training courses offered by suppliers to help gain more of an understanding of passenger vehicles and how they worked. After two years, the company Braeden worked at before offered him another contract. I was so grateful. I was hopeful that this would help fix things at home.

A year into the contract, Braeden suggested we buy a bigger house, and I agreed only on the condition of us developing and sticking to a budget. We bought a beautiful home in the suburbs in a great area for our daughter. Only three months later, he was laid off; but I thought we were good. We had managed to put away a decent nest egg that we could use to help with expenses. Then, while I was out of town, he spent it all on a new truck, and financed the difference. He did this on the day before his official start-day of his layoff. Any sliver of trust that I had vanished that day.

By 2005, my marriage was over. We couldn't talk without arguing, and I was constantly exhausted. He made it clear that if I left, *"I would have nothing, and would be nothing."* I believed every word. After all, my mother told me the same thing. I sought out the advice of a lawyer, but it still took me a year-and-a-half to actually make the move and leave. I was terrified, tired, and burned out. When I told him that I didn't think that there was enough left to work on, and that I thought we really needed to consider moving on, his answer was *"Well, that's just great. Now I'm going to have to sell my new truck because I can't afford to pay you child support and keep it."* I remember thinking, *"If that was his gut reaction to his wife and child leaving, he was likely trying to stay for the same wrong reasons."*

The day I went to the attorney to start the process, the unthinkable happened. The owner of the property that housed the garage, gave me a ninety-day notice of eviction. They decided to revamp the property to include a large convenience store, instead of my shop. So, while starting divorce proceedings, I was also looking to re-locate the business. I was terrified that I could potentially end up homeless, jobless, and a single parent. And Braeden was always in the background, threatening to do whatever it took to make that a reality.

Chase The Vision

We can feel sorry for ourselves
or we can put the work boots on and
understand the situation and the reality of it all.

Marty Turco

There was no time or energy to feel sorry for myself. I knew that the key was to be proactive. After all of the things I had already gone through, I was determined more than ever that I wouldn't let all of the hard work and challenges get to me.

This was a pivotal point where I had to re-evaluate what I truly wanted. I seriously considered closing the business, so the costs of closing it down were absorbed into the divorce. I had choices and decisions to make: I could start a new business, even one out of the automotive industry, or even find a *"real job"* where I would have benefits, pension, and a steady income. But I decided to stick with it. I had a vision of what I wanted the company to be.

It was that vision that had me out evenings and weekends leaving notes taped to large industrial buildings in our area looking for space to lease. The same vision that had me calling every person I knew in the local automotive industry to put the word out that I was looking for space. Soon, a real estate agent approached me about leasing a site north of our small town, and so with only nine days to go until our leaving the property, I signed the lease. I spent the next nine days putting up as much signage as possible to let everyone know where we were headed. I received a note from my grandmother telling me how brave I was and how proud she was of me. I knew I made the right choice.

If I was going to make this work, one thing was for certain, I was going to have to put it *all on the line*. Life was changing dramatically for me at this time. I wanted to be the granddaughter that my grandmother would be proud of, and a good role model for my daughter. While I didn't always feel like I was capable, I looked and back and realized just how far I had already come without any real business knowledge or experience. So now that I had experience, I thought to myself, *"How far can I take this?"*

New Dreams And Beginnings

Once the shop moved, it was time to secure a place to live. I found a small apartment close to our marital home, so my daughter could continue to go to the same school, and stay with her same crew of friends. After my less than stable childhood, Kendall was my first priority. I was adamant that, regardless of how Braeden treated me, I was going to make whatever sacrifices I needed to.

Within a year, we finalized the divorce settlement and custody arrangements. My first weekend without my daughter was tough. I spent a lot of time thinking about how many families do this, and the feelings that come with your marriage ending. I started to think about my own upbringing, and how my dad must have felt thirty years before when he walked away from almost all of his possessions, and his kids. After a few months, I reached out to my dad for the first time in almost twenty years. He was very open and welcoming to healing our relationship; it's a decision that I have never regretted.

I also found a small run down house in the area that I was able to purchase and fix up for us to live in. I was officially a single mom, and sole proprietor. Just in time for a global economic downturn. Brave or stupid, I soldiered on.

Learning The Business Ropes

I'm a steel-toed boots
in a ballet-slipper world.

Richard Kadrey

Being in a male-dominated industry has come with many challenges and it has pushed me to through my comfort zone on so many levels. I decided that one of the ways to learn and grow was to *listen.* I listened to every opportunity and idea, regardless of how unrelated or *"out there"* it sounded. When sales reps would cold call, I would listen to their sales pitch instead of immediately dismissing them. I would read mass emails, and ask sales reps for new products. I also had to change how I viewed spending money within the company. Instead of focusing on the bills, costs and finances, I needed to look at what each dollar spent could mean in revenue for the company. Instead of looking at new equipment purchases and upgrades as another monthly expense, I asked how much more work and income could each new piece generate? I knew I could make the business not only good, but great.

At this point, I had to start with bringing in any and all work I could, and to find these clients, I needed to advertise. How can I stand out without it being costly? Big advertising campaigns are expensive, and money wasn't plentiful. So I tried a lot of new small ideas. Anything that I could. I talked to current clients, especially self-employed ones, looking for advice and ideas.

A client offered to get me on local television through his nephew. So, I spent some time on local television as their automotive representative, giving automotive tips and advice to viewers. Not only did it advertise our location, but I made some networking connections. The TV station executives actually reached out to me personally about putting together a television show for them, but I decided that the timing wasn't right.

I started writing a *"brochure"* of commonly asked questions for my clients. It turned into a one hundred and thirty page book. I decided to reach out to some editors in our trade magazines, and one agreed to meet me. He was very helpful, informative, and gave me a few options. Then he offered me a position writing for a magazine he was preparing to publish bi-yearly. I agreed, and, in 2008, I started writing in *Canadian Car Owner* magazine. I continued to do that for two years.

Things at the new location weren't as busy as the old one. Because of the distance between my old location, and this new one, we did lose some clientele. That's when the economy fell hard. People didn't have the money to spend, and if they did, they were buying brand new, because the car companies were almost giving them away at cost. I did everything I could to survive, but with only one income at home, I struggled. I ended up in more debt than I had ever imagined. By late 2009, I decided if I was going to survive, I needed to downsize. Since my clientele had been downsized, I figured downsizing the size of the company was a viable option.

I found a small industrial condominium unit back in our small town for sale. I refinanced my house to use as a down payment, and managed to talk the owner of the unit into holding a mortgage for the difference. While it increased my house mortgage payment by $44 a month, my business expenses dropped by $2500 a month, and I owned my location, instead of being at the mercy of commercial landlords. I was scared, but I could see the vision and believed. I moved in 2010. I had such a limited budget because of the current downturn that any big expensive marketing was out of the question. My old landlord refused to let me put up any signage. So I sat down and spent a Saturday calling each customer I could to let them know of our move.

The beauty of any small town is the lightning speed of word of mouth. Things were looking up, but didn't turn around immediately, of course, and unfortunately I ended up laying off some of my staff. The tech that I did have had an active family life and was away quite a bit. So being the only person in the building when he was gone, I decided the best way to keep things rolling was to figure this car stuff out myself.

The Internet Working For Or Against You

When I heard about the first viral bad internet review about a company, I was shocked. I remember thinking that, *"This was the type of thing that could really wreck a company's reputation."* Many auto shop reviews pointed out a lack of cleanliness, bad language, and a very unfriendly atmosphere. That is when I realized the power of marketing on the internet. I've always been a people pleaser. It was part of who I was, but I took that quality and made it about my business. So with any customer complaint, I looked at it as an opportunity to turn it into advertising for our customer service. I made sure our office was clean and inviting. The biggest thing I did and still do today, regardless of what is going on around me, is that I greet everyone that comes through the door a big smile and *"Hello!"* Seems simple, but in the automotive industry, it's rarer than most realize.

I spent a lot of time reading other garages posted reviews. Often, a Google or social media review will outline a problem or issue that the client felt they had with the company. I would look at each of those and compare to our set up, to try to ensure that we wouldn't have the same complaints wherever possible. Fair pricing, happy positive atmosphere, and quality workmanship became our big three goals.

The Broad Behind The Counter: Business And Personal Growth

I have heard it all, and truthfully I have been referred to as *"The Broad Behind The Counter."* People who are not familiar with me and my garage would ask to speak to the owner, assuming that I wasn't because, I was a woman. They think that I am the receptionist.

Years of overseeing the technicians as they worked, and answering questions for clientele, while attending training seminars had given me a good amount of knowledge. I felt that I needed the official schooling. I started to book simple work for when I was alone, like oil changes, tire changes, and tire repairs. I spent two nights a week in trade school at the local college. When Kendall wasn't home, I spent my weekends at work, trying to build the company and improve the space. I had one technician working for me, and I ran between the office and the shop. I still stayed late periodically, when my daughter was otherwise engaged.

As things improved, I hired a second technician. I focused on the business side of things, doing all I could to attract clients. I had a coffee date with a friend in marketing, and took two very important things away from it:

1. What made me different from my competitors is what I should be accentuating.

2. Why was I investing my marketing money, time and energy into promoting jobs that were loss leaders?

It seemed so simple, yet was the beginning of such a revolution in my head. I had always been a wallflower, but *"The Broad Behind The Counter"* was about to become the center of the marketing plan. I decided to try lawn bag signs and spent weekends running signs in the high traffic areas. I also looked to social media to help gain clients. When it started working, and the cash flow improved, I started a radio campaign on local radio station. As it gained in popularity, I moved the ads to a station with a larger audience reach. With the better cash flow, I could afford to ask myself, *"How much business will this generate?"* instead of *"How much will this cost?"*

Love Turns Up

A friend of mine ran a coffee truck service and would come by the shop daily. She repeatedly suggested that it was time for me to start dating—and she had a friend to introduce me to. After a month, I agreed to meet her friend, Steve, for coffee.

The coffee date went well and Steve and I started dating. I discovered that Steve was so different than anyone I had ever met before. He was motivated, dynamic, had a great attitude; nothing seemed to stop him. Steve jumped in feet first to help with anything he could, whether it was fixing my house, helping at work, or even spending time with Kendall when I couldn't. He had two amazing kids of his own, and soon they all moved into my house.

Steve's career was pretty solid. He was also one of those guys who is pretty handy with just about anything and he was business savvy. Steve started helping out at work and even came up with solutions to financial challenges that arose. I knew that he was exactly what the company needed. I couldn't run both the back and the front at the same time. After years of suggesting it, he finally came on board. That was five years ago, and even through COVID, we managed to grow.

Since then, our garage has tripled in space, and sales now are twelve times what they were ten years ago. To stay to my roots and management style, I can still be found at the front counter every day.

Keeping The Dream Alive

Mindset and keeping with my vision have been the biggest game changers for me. Focus, drive, and determination have pushed me through the tough times. These virtues are also what gave me the confidence and permission to grow. I managed to keep coming up with new and innovative processes, things I wouldn't have done, had I not been determined to keep the dream alive. Even on the brink of professional and personal collapse, I focused on where I wanted to be. I chased that vision with all that I had. To get to the top, you have to be prepared for unexpected roadblocks, learn to do your best to prevent them, and be prepared to navigate them. When the negativity and doubt set in, I learned to take that energy and re-invest it in building my brand. I learned that if you take every bit of negativity to heart, you will eventually flatline. Instead, send that negativity to your feet, and use it as a stepstool to help reach your goal.

Through it all, I am continuing my growth journey, both personally and professionally. I strive to be better for myself and others each and every day. I do my best to create that work-life balance and enjoy family time. I get involved and give back to my community through charity events and sponsorship both personally and include my *"work family"* as well. These are the things that feed my soul. In business, my automotive service business is no different than any other business. The focus is on *service*. I am not *just* servicing someone's vehicle, I am serving the customer. It is the experience that matters. I always look inward and ask myself, *"How can I make a difference today?" "How can I make my customers feel happy and welcomed, adding value in their service experience?"* This introspection has been the key to *not only* keep my dream alive but has allowed me, my personal life, and my business to thrive.

Chase the vision, not the money.
The money will end up following you.

Tony Hsieh

We may encounter many defeats,
but we must not be defeated.

Maya Angelou

Sandra Lisi

Sandra Lisi is a published author, philanthropist, Canadian Women in Leadership award recipient, leadership coach for women, Founder of Sandra in the Sity and Co-Founder of The Sity Society which is her non-profit organization. She has a 'get shit done' attitude which has been her motto while climbing in both the private and public sectors. Sandra's journey to executive levels came with many challenges both professionally and personally but her perseverance and focus kept her going. Leading, inspiring, mentoring and creating an impact are what keeps her soul fueled with passion and purpose.

Finding My Nama

Sandra Lisi

If you get a chance, take it.
If it changes your life, let it.
Nobody said it'd be easy,
they just promised it
would be worth it

Dr. Suess

"You are such a good girl!" were words that I always strived to hear. Being the first generation and oldest child in an Italian family, I was always the good kid. I abided by the rules, listened to my parents, *"no"* meant *"no,"* and didn't cross the line. I may have tried, but I knew the limits. That was me: the good girl who tried her best to do well in school, help around the house, learn domestic tasks, and take care of her younger brother—you know, the usual stuff that doesn't land you in trouble, grounded, or frozen by *"the stare."*

Our middle-class working family lived in an affluent area; however, we were not like most families in the area. I was the oldest of two kids and both of my parents worked. My parents tried to never deprive us of anything, but in reality, I still didn't have enough stuff to be part of the *"cool kid"* crowd in school. While I did have many friends, I didn't fit in. I was in the *"second circle,"* the outsiders that hung out together at school, on weekends, and at parties. As a teenager, being an outsider wasn't the circle you wanted to be in.

These things bothered me and sometimes they felt like the biggest problems in the world. At that age not being asked to dance at the school dance was heart crushing and the stress of being sure you were wearing the latest fashions on "Casual Fridays" was like having a burning stomach-ache as Fridays crept closer. I was glad I went to a Catholic school and wore a uniform, so I didn't have to worry about fashion from Monday to Thursday. This is the age when the limiting belief of *"not enough"* starts to set in: not good enough, not pretty enough, not skinny enough, not cool enough... all the enoughs!

Decades later I realized that the *"enoughs"* continued. As an adult I was constantly seeking validation from others through acceptance, whether it was with friendships, relationships, my bosses, or society as a whole. The school years are a critical time for building self-worth and self-esteem.

Adulting Is Overrated

Being done with academics so that I could be *"grown-up"* was all I wanted. I couldn't wait to be part of the working world. I looked forward to adult-life where I could make my own decisions, live my life my way, and do whatever I wanted. I soon learned becoming an adult is so overrated. Thinking back, *"Why did I want to rush through one of the most carefree periods of my life?"* However, so many of us wanted that. The grass is never greener on the other side. Truth is, the grass is greener where you water it.

My mom always says I was born without patience. I know that about myself. After rushing through school, I continued my rush to become a grown-up by rushing to find a full-time, *"secure"* job and then into marriage. A few hard life lessons from this rushing knocked me on my ass and forced me to learn to take my time when making major decisions.

Playing It Safe

As a daughter of a bank teller, it was only fitting that my summer jobs and then full-time work were in banking. It was thought of as *"a good and secure job,"* so why wouldn't I choose it? I was hungry to learn and I enjoyed being in a service-based industry. It was natural that it made me feel all grown-up, and that I was moving into adulthood exactly as I had planned. I started to re-alize that leading others was something that came naturally to me as throughout high school and college I had coached a girls soccer team in our community and taught catechism at our local church. I never really gave much thought to the fact that I was a natural born leader until I entered the workforce full-time and paid attention to these traits.

My hunger to learn had me watching, learning, and studying behaviors like how people spoke to their colleagues and to their customers, and how managers carried themselves and presented themselves. I wanted to be a manager some day and then *"a big boss"*—and, oh boy, I knew that when I made the *"big bucks"* I would feel great enough to jump over the moon.

I entered the workforce in the early 1990s. Being a woman and making a *decent salary* in a male dominated industry was a stark reality at the time. Women were not considered *"good enough"* to make as much as men for the same or equal job. This inequality still exists today.

Through my early years in banking, I was doing well professionally but personally I was a bit of mess. I did all the right things according to my environment: I got an education, got married, bought a house, had a good job and *that was supposed to be it*. Life was all set. Ah no, not for me it wasn't. While I lived the *"expectations"* from an exterior perspective, I struggled so much internally with this. I felt suffocated in my personal life, living a traditional suburban married life as this was the expectation from my Italian culture, but inside I just wanted to be Carrie Bradshaw from *Sex and the City*. Needless to say, the marriage ended and with that came a personal bankruptcy and some truly humbling experiences that I had to face. This shit got real very fast.

My mindset had shifted because my circumstances changed. However, it forced me to go introspectively, delve into my unconscious mind and understand my journey thus far. I knew that I needed to change if I wanted my life to change for the better. I felt one thing was certain: I was not going to stay busted and broke. I still had my career and I was going to focus on me doing well and moving up. The dreams that I had for *me* may have been stalled and detoured, but they were not going to die. I was going to get the big job, buy the condo, get the car I always wanted, take the trips, and buy those bags!

So, what seemed to turn my life upside down actually turned my life right side up. I had two jobs after the divorce and a bankruptcy from marital debt. My first job was at the bank and I took on the second job with a local small business. That second job really opened my eyes to entrepreneurship. I learned a lot about the art of building business relationships, the hustling of deals (which we now call the art of negotiations), about what *not to do*, and those pitfalls that small businesses need to really be aware of. The biggest lessons I learned from this experience was that I could do whatever I set my mind to. I watched someone succeed despite having just immigrated to Canada with English as a second language, not a very nice person and yet, savvy in business. If they could do it, why couldn't I?

Through all of this, I was committed to the vision I had for my life. I was determined and kept going. There were roadblocks along the way with emotional struggles and pain. These allowed me to develop the courage to start planning and working towards the life I had envisioned for myself and not the life that others expected of me. I was determined not to allow these experiences, people, and challenges stop me from being who I truly am and going after what I really wanted. This is where I began to learn patience, mindfulness, and planning. Self-care became critical, not selfish. Self-care for me was not just facials and manicures, but more in the sense of therapy, faith, and personal development. I turned my focus to my self-awakening journey. This is what got me to where I am today and I am damn proud!

The moment I moved from manager to the senior management levels was glorious. Let me tell you, you know that happy dance you do when no one is watching? Yep, mid-thirties and I was killing it professionally. I had broken ties with anything and anyone holding me back personally. I started to thrive in my own skin, my confidence was at its all time high, and the fruits of my hard work had started to show. I no longer needed the part-time job. I bought my condo in the City, got my new car, and was free from all of my past. I paid my dues and now I was living the life I had envisioned, the life I wanted and all on my own terms.

Sometimes those life-humbling moments are awful and the struggle is hard but in those lowest of low moments, I made the decision that I would never spend my last ten dollars, and I would no longer tolerate anyone putting me down and tell me I was not good enough. I stopped searching for external acceptance and focused on the road to emotional and mental liberation. You see, those experiences and feelings we have as children and into our youth stay with us and do impact us. It was only when I stopped to acknowledge all of these feelings and understood them that I was able to start to move past them.

I Saw My Worth

Determination kept me focused on my career and the next role, however, limiting beliefs held me back. That little voice inside my head—you know the one that talks us out of stepping outside of our comfort zones. All the things that I didn't have professionally that I thought I needed to have, truly kept me at a certain level until it didn't.

One of the things I have always done is to look at the work I was interested in doing next. I would assess what skills I needed to build, what I needed to improve on, then start incorporating those skills and improvements into my current position. I did this so that when that next role came available, I would be ready.

I would be able to demonstrate the skills, provide the examples, and apply those to the new role. If you can't gain the skills you need for the next promotion in your current role, you may need to move laterally to a role that will help you gain them. But again, I only applied to roles that were *"in my range"* or more like what my limiting beliefs told me I could do.

I have had many *bosses* throughout my career and I use the term *bosses*, as not all of them were *leaders*. However, I learned from each and every one of them. From the great ones, I took their wonderful qualities and from the shitty ones, well, you learn what not to do. But from everyone, I *learned* and that is the key.

One of the great leaders I had the pleasure of working for once asked me what seemed to me to be a really odd question. He asked me why I did not have anything to say in his management meetings. I thought deeply about this and realized he may have interpreted my quietness as a lack of knowledge, insight, and who knows what else. That was furthest from the truth. It was a new team I joined and I was hired because of all the knowledge and skills I brought to the role and this team.

My quiet demeanour was my lack of self-confidence, not my lack of knowledge. It was not my lack of skills but *me*—that feeling of not being good enough was surfacing up again and now it was showing big time. My boss had noticed it. You see, I was surrounded by peers who had way more education than I did and I felt intimidated. I discounted the value I brought to the team because I felt less than them. Not because I was, but because that is how I felt. No one ever made me feel that way. I did that all to myself. This *aha* moment hit me hard because I didn't want the impression of me being unengaged to continue. That is when my vocal cords warmed up and I started sharing, engaging, and being a part of the team. I spoke to add value, to share my experiences, providing innovation, suggestions, and contributing. Let me tell you, that was a huge turning point for me and I felt so empowered in my own skin. So much so, that I had a kick-ass year and was viewed as high performing and of high potential by the organization. I was now in a position to have the organization find me the next role and not the other way around.

It Doesn't Have To Be Lonely At The Top

Through all of these roles I have always been a leader of people. I managed teams, deliverables, targets and objectives to produce results. I built a reputation for myself as the *"girl who gets shit done"* as one of my incredible leaders named me. She believed in me. She encouraged me to do more, be more, offering me the support that I, as a leader, provided to my team. So, the *"get shit done girl"* continuously developed my team to be filled with high performing individuals who through coaching, mentoring, confidence, and skill building were then known as the *"get results team."*

Moving up the ranks is rewarding and uncomfortable at the same time. The chase has your adrenaline running high and then the catch is you now having to deliver. That is when the rubber hits the road. There is no greater feeling than to realize how far you have come and how grateful you are. Oftentimes, as people climb the ladder, their humility decreases. One of the most important traits of a great leader is their humbleness and their desire to continue to be of service: service to their team, their company, the public, and themselves. The top can be a lonely place if you do not bring others along with you.

Trust Needs To Be Earned

In 2018, I found myself, for the first time, in a position where I could make a change in my career. I was considering a career outside of the financial services life I had known for over twenty years, where I had *"grown-up."* My so-called *"safe space."* I had been feeling stuck for a long time and my limiting beliefs held me back from making bold moves. I stopped myself from venturing into work that I was truly passionate about, work that had a greater impact on the lives of others. Those *"not enough"* beliefs held me back and I guess the Universe had been listening for all those years when I would think, *"Ok, what's next?"*

I finally felt I was at the right place and mindset to believe in myself and take bold steps in the direction of my purpose and passion. There was change happening in all aspects of my life, both personally and professionally. To say things were somewhat unstable would be an understatement but in hindsight, it was what I needed to go through to come out on the other side. I worked with a professional coach because even the coach needs a coach, to figure out what was next. This was by far one of the best moments of my life where I was able to focus on what I truly wanted to do and how the hell I was going to do it. The benefits of having a professional coach to help you figure this all out is that they can try to make sense of your chaos.

Coaching was an outside fresh perspective that helped; it led me down the path to my self-discovery of my life's next chapter: the birth of "Sandra in the Sity." I discovered my passion and purpose in life, where I could bring to light all of the rises and falls, all the lessons learned, the experiences and the guts it took to go from surviving to thriving. I created a leadership coaching practice that helped women like myself move through their limiting beliefs both personally and professionally. It gave me a feeling of pride seeing these women overcome and own who they are beyond their *"stuckness"* and thrive.

Setting My Own Bar

I needed to move away from my limiting thoughts to shining my light. I changed paths from the corporate world to public service life. I determined that working in government is where I could make more of an impact on the lives of others.

Life as a public servant leader, in particular over the past three years, has been some of the most rewarding work of my entire career. Leading during the global COVID-19 pandemic, a time of so much uncertainty, change, and volatility, has allowed me to demonstrate all of the traits, skills, commitment, and strength I have. I had to show this not only to the people I lead, but also to the largest municipality in Canada—to its residents, businesses, and tourists.

I Found My Nama

Had my journey not been as it was, my limiting beliefs would have continued to hold me back and this story may have been different. I moved into a new sector in my late forties as well as my entrepreneurial journey as a coach. My personal life turned out exactly how I had envisioned it many years before. I finally found my perfect life partner as he encourages me, my growth and my journey. This was worth every struggle, failure, and heartbreak as it allowed me to become the woman I am today.

Part of my life of service is to provide for women and children who are less fortunate than I am. Like most, I donated to campaigns and fundraisers. But during the pandemic, I wanted to do more, and in particular for women and children of domestic abuse. The lockdowns were tough on most people, but can you imagine being in lockdown with your abuser? That really pulled on my heart strings and I thought hard about how I could help those women. Women who leave their abusers and show up on the doorsteps of shelters with nothing but the clothes on their backs and often with children in tow.

With this thought, I ran a campaign on social media for the month of February 2021 which I called *"The Love For All Women."* We collected non-perishable food, personal hygiene products, gift cards, and money for the women and children living in a local women's shelter in my area. The results surpassed my expectations as the overwhelming support from so many, near and far, was incredible. We were able to not only provide what the shelter needed for the women and children they supported, but also to shine a ray of hope in their lives. We wanted these survivors to know we saw them as worthy and enough; we wanted them to know they are loved. And that was only the start.

My burning passion to be of service to others led to another one of my visions coming to life—the creation of a non-profit organization for women and children of domestic abuse. The Sity Society was born in January 2021. It is my first non-profit organization, created with five incredible co-founders. Together we have been able to impact the lives of women and children living in four women's shelters in the Greater Toronto and Hamilton, Ontario areas in Canada. We have plans to take The Sity Society across Canada in the next five years.

We have the ability to make an impact on the lives of others and that is what I have set out to do in my life. The journey to finding my NAMA has not been a straight line; it has been a journey filled with gratitude, impact, passion, and purpose.

Tune into your truth.
Live it. Breathe it. Beam it.

Emma Kate

Passion first, and everything else
will fall into place.

Holly Holm

Dr. Kim Redman

Dr. Kim Redman is a visionary, Founder and CEO of Creatrix Go Quantum, Keynote Speaker, Multiple #1 International Best Selling Author, Global Expert, Board Designated Master Trainer and Quantum Stage Goddess. She is Canada's Board Designated Master Trainer in NLP, Hypnosis, Time Line Therapy® and NLP Results Coaching. For over thirty years, Dr. Kim has been passionate about working with Conscious Entrepreneurs who want to break concrete ceilings and helps launch them nationally and internationally into crazy success.

Goddess Unleashed™

Dr. Kim Redman

*As women we've been programmed to sacrifice everything
in the name of what is good and right for everyone else.
Then if there's an inch left over, maybe we can
have a piece of that. We need to deprogram ourselves.*

Oprah Winfrey

I am no stranger to life's challenges both personally and profession-ally. Living through and overcoming numerous obstacles gave me the fuel to understand that nothing is impossible; abandonment, death by strangulation (I came back), a cervical spine injury that left a hairline crack in C2 and ligament damage, cervical cancer, rehabbing for a year to learn how to walk again, and other injuries too numerous to list. I would venture to say, there were many more elegant ways to learn some of the lessons of my journey. In the depths of darkness, I found the Light of my Inner Goddess. The Goddess relationship is still one of the most important relationships in my life and it continues to evolve as I evolve. It is compassionate, heart-based, and sustainable. It also requires saying no, without apology, anger, or explanation. That too is a powerful gift.

At many points throughout my exponential growth experiences I needed to re-engage with those lessons. I thought that my tools were enough. I couldn't believe my direction had slid backwards to fueling others rather than *"paying myself first."* Some lessons are universal and constant. The Universe always brings what we need so we can harness the Goddess within and serve through our highest self.

Everything I envisioned and prayed for in my business and life to be, had manifested. I had learned that we are *"God-spark."* According to all esoteric, philosophy, mysticism, and quantum physics, we create our realities. As I like to say from the stage, *"Welcome to Life School. It's called Planet Earth University. How's it going so far?"* So why did I wind up here, now?

Surrender, Release, Re-Evaluate

As you grow older, you will discover that you have two hands, one for helping yourself, the other for helping others.

Maya Angelou

I had reached the *definition* of success. My company was rocking it and was considered to be *the* country's leader in our industry. My marriage was amazing. I mentored others and poured my heart and soul into our graduate community. By all accounts, *I had it all*. It's what society defines as success. However, none of it was sustainable.

The Universe was tapping me on both shoulders. I was too busy to see it or feel it, until my soul screamed so loudly that my body started to shut down. My immune system was on the verge of collapsing and I was exhausted. Diagnosed with adrenal fatigue, I began to see the signs of cancer showing up in my life *again. And no one knew it.*

I felt overwhelmed and conflicted. I mean, isn't *this* what everyone wants? Others look to me as their mentor, a role model. They want to achieve what I have accomplished. My goal has been to help each of my students and graduates to reach their pinnacle level of success. I questioned myself repeatedly about this. *"How did I wind up here?! Hadn't I learned the lessons about over-taxing myself before? All that healing work, studying with shamans and naturopaths, and the International META-Medicine Association. Why was I revisiting this set of lessons again?"*

A meltdown led to a beautiful surrender moment. I reached out to one of my mentors, and just vented it all. Two cups of tea and half a box of tissues later, she asked me one question that totally changed my perspective. *"So… is it bad enough for you to change it or just bitch about it?"* Good question. I sat back, took a deep breath and pondered for a bit. My mind was reeling with my own fear-based questions. *"If I changed how I did things would my success stop? Would my contribution to my family and my mission be negatively impacted? Would my clients (or friends) leave if I wasn't ever-and-always available?"*

I asked her for advice, *"What do I do?"*

"Well," she said, *"The first thing that you have to do is put YOU into the mix. You and your needs aren't even in the conversation. The when I... then I... approach has failed."*

Wow. She was right. It hadn't even occurred to me to have that conversation. Right there, is the beauty of a mentor. The truth was, that this level of success was new for me. I realized that I didn't have a clue how to *have it all.* I had grown. My company had grown and *yet* my strategies, resources and behavior had not grown with me, at least not at the same speed. I was attempting to live in a new place, with old strategies. I hadn't realized that I was only using leftovers for myself. Once I had that clarity from my mentor, I realized what steps I had to take. I needed to get back to myself, to surrender, release the fears and re-evaluate my health, mindset and business.

You can't run a car without fuel. Have you ever tried to balance a bicycle when it's not moving? It's the movement or flow that allows balance to happen. It's a dynamic action, and we usually think of balance as a static state. It's not. Since there is no such thing as balance, how do we generate the fluidity and sustainability that we require for dynamic action?

Balance is an illusion. As many of us strive for *"success,"* one of the pitfalls to entrepreneurship can be how easily we can get caught up on that hamster wheel, constantly looking forward and outward instead of also looking within. It is easy to get caught up and fall into that trap.

> *Balance is the epiphany that you don't have*
> *to be everything to everyone, all of the time.*
>
> **Vanessa Autrey**

Passion And Purpose

I always say that your passion will lead you to your purpose. Cautionary note: Passion is a fuel. Like all fuel it can launch a spacecraft, or blow up on the launch pad. As I rejected the traditional lessons of womanhood and family, I followed my heart.

I was seeking freedom from the constraints I brought with me. Seeking to escape my own internal programming. Seeking to *"make a change."* What change this was I had no idea, but I believed then that wanting it was enough. *It's not, by the way.* I was seeking affirmation externally that I was good enough, or worth enough, to belong to a tribe after the abandonment of my family. I was seeking answers as to how these scenarios could have happened to a loved, planned child. I was seeking to find how to heal and change the world.

In reality, I was seeking how to heal and change *me*, but I didn't know that consciously at the time. My Higher Self, the Divine, and it seemed the Universe, were in on the plan. They assisted me in creating the perfect situations to reveal the answers that I was seeking. The answers needed unwrapping though, and that took some time.

Quantum Reality

As we say in Neuro Linguistic Programming or NLP, *"Your focus creates your behavior, and your behavior creates your results."* Choose wisely. Action to shift what is out of balance and your body and life will follow. That's called an *'actionable focus'* in coaching. The lesson here is that you have to *"get real"* about what you feel, if you want to heal.

LESSON 1:

You are a hologram. Quantum physics speculates that the whole Universe is a hologram. This means that everything we think, feel, and do, impacts everything else. It is lunacy to believe that your work-life doesn't impact your home-life and vice versa. It does because it impacts your biology and wherever you go, there you are! This is also how we get the most bang for our buck... any asset we add into the system, benefits the whole system. *Everywhere.*

LESSON 2:

Your biology doesn't *"think"* about how you feel. Actually it doesn't care what you think at all. It cares what you believe, how you feel, and whether or not you perceive that you have choice in your life. It's the ultimate feedback mechanism. Your biology responds to the environment outside of you, and the environment between your ears.

I would speculate that the world inside your head is even more impactful than the world outside of us, because we carry that inner Universe with us, everywhere. Then we project *"the way it is"* onto the world around us, creating self-fulfilling prophecies. Life happens. The meaning we give those events is up to us. Whatever methods you use, shamanism, NLP, psychology, know that they all work. Please learn the tools to change your inside world. It's the best way to create the world you were born to thrive in.

LESSON 3:

You always have choice. If you can't see or hear those choices, if you can't wrap your head around the fact that there is a choice, then by definition you have a gap. The solution is to reach out to somebody *solution-minded* quickly. I will readily admit that in acknowledging those choices, you may need to let go of being right, in order to reach happy, healthy and wealthy. Success does breed success. The more, happy, healthy and wealthy we get, the less we care about being right. Set up your outside environment in whatever ways you can to support your happy, healthy and wealthy self.

Quantum Success

Living joyfully is an art because joy is subjective and unique to each of us. Abundance, money and success are all based on a recipe, and skills.

I am a talented person. It took years to build skills. Talented people want it all yesterday. In my healing I needed to learn that the shamans say, *"It is done, when it is done,"* for a reason. I needed to surrender; to the Divine, to the process, to the mission of being in service, and that meant surrendering the need to do it alone. Surrender is part of success, and it's still a challenging lesson for me. I know if it's hard, I'm doing it wrong. If I get a result, I am doing it right. It's a pretty simple philosophy, but it doesn't mean it is easy.

Right now we are in a *'bridging time'* between science and spirit, between past and future, between the *"haves"* and *"have nots."* We have the opportunity to create a society that supports us all. This bridging time allows us to synthesize ideologies and concepts, and easily synergize new techniques.

LESSON 1:

All resistance, hardship and obstacles are there because we need to learn something. This something can be a skill set, a behavior, or an ideology that stretches us beyond our comfort zone. Growth begins at the end of the comfort zone. Change is inevitable, and growth is a choice. Your ego will get an initial bashing, and then magic will happen.

LESSON 2:

The Universe is perfect even if I am not. This means that all things do really happen for a reason. I am the reason, and if I can get the learning and the *"aha"* then I can move into gratitude. The lesson will make your Universe a much better place to be.

LESSON 3:

Seek out success recipes. Seek out mentorship. Seek out coaches. It makes success a party and gives you a pick me up when it's hard. A good mentor will share with you their secret recipes. We all need someone to guide us around the big potholes, or at least help inch our way out of the hole! Keep asking until it vibes with you. You deserve it. Question if someone has already done what you are seeking to do, and go get *their* recipe. It allows us to get the happy, healthy and wealthy so much faster than before.

The Interdependent Goddess Mindset

"I can do it myself." "Why bother to ask anyone, by the time I explain it, I could just do it myself…" These are statements of mental, emotional, physical, spiritual, and financial poverty. Thoughts of this nature happen in a survival mentality, not a thriving Goddess

Mindset mentality. One of the things I have learned along the way from growing a company into a seven figure business, is that independence has a very low concrete ceiling. Yes, it's concrete, not glass. Tapping into our independent mindset gives us a win-lose scope. You have an opponent. It is poverty and competition based.

Interdependence is a win-win-win phenomena; you win, they win and the relationship wins. Interdependence also functions on reciprocity. A relationship is a dynamic system. Reciprocity requires that a system receives more than it gives. Any system that gives out more than it receives, dies. This is the natural order of things.

I believe many of today's Goddesses are in a type of spiritual grieving because we need to be plugged into something bigger than ourselves, something we can give to and receive from. We are natural nurturers. We also need to remember that we are natural receivers, and when we refuse to receive, than we deprive someone else of the gift of giving. This behavior stops the flow of reciprocity and is wildly unproductive.

Many of us need to find and create a tribe outside of our family unit, either in addition to, or in place of the original family unit. As a business woman, and/or entrepreneur, this takes on a whole new scope. I recommend finding a mastermind group, mentor, or coach who has demonstrated that they are sustainably where you want to be. Interdependence helps you avoid many pitfalls.

Goddess Consciousness

What we think about and value becomes our consciousness. It is through our perceptions that we create our reality. If we have a limiting belief about something, that becomes our truth. Shifting and embracing our Goddess consciousness to achieve success in life and business takes deep introspection. How do you tap into *your* Goddess consciousness? Perception is key with regard to gratitude, balance, time and money.

GRATITUDE

I have found that opening up the *stream of goodness* is key. I suggest the amazing tool of *'gratituding.'* Ask yourself, how well do I receive a compliment? Do I accept it easily, or brush it off? Do I easily ask for help? How bad does it have to be before I reach out for help? Gratituding is a great way to shift this stuck energy. Write down 5 things every day that actually happened that opened your heart.

BALANCE

Balance, or the movement between the different areas of our lives takes awareness, planning, and practice. Time is never truly the issue, although it is a symptom of lack of balance and boundaries. Both productive and unproductive people have the same number of hours in a day. Efficiency around time is really the skill set we all need to develop. That's why in business you will often hear, *"Give it to a busy person. they will get it done."*

TIME

Time is a commodity. That means that it can't be saved, it can only be spent. I thought I understood time management because I had a busy life, my *"stuff"* got done, and I was on time. Nope. Managing time by spending it on the most important things allows for greater focus, prioritization, and the freedom to take advantage of opportunities that present themselves.

MONEY

"I want to, but I just don't have the money." We have all said this at one time or another. The real questions around money as a resource can bring up some uncomfortable truths. Money is our symbol of value in this society. According to behavior and coaching tenets, if we will spend money on others, but not self, then that indicates a problem with how we value ourselves. If we spend money on self, without awareness of how those choices impact other people and areas of our lives, then that's retail therapy and a short termed dopamine hit. It's not a sustainable lifestyle.

Money terrified me earlier in my life. Money was attached to some of my experiences around trauma. Even thinking about spending money used to leave me in a pile of tears, incapable of functioning. My life mission was important to me, and in order to live my mission, I needed to learn money management and wealth management strategies. NLP and Time Line Therapy® assisted me in removing the PTSD around the traumas, and the tribe of my husband, friends and mentors supported me as I learned.

One day, I viscerally realized that money was an energy of exchange. Completely neutral. After that mindset shift, money is now an empowering experience for me and I enjoy sharing what I have learned.

Connection And Communication: The How To

The first connection that we need to source is the connection to ourselves and our own unconscious minds. The fastest way to balance is to clear out, and realign all of the conflicting programs that are ping-ponging around our own minds. You know what I mean, it's the negative self-talk and chaos we all have.

Learning to program the programmable parts of ourselves is an essential part of creating more of the healthy, balanced, sourced world that we seek. I have seen the shocking difference in my life, in my clients lives, and the ripple effects that move through families, businesses, and societies. Positivity begets positivity and success calls to greater success. My company is part of my giveback. Assisting people into balance and more magnificent versions of themselves feeds my soul. It is a process that leaves me humbled, awed, and gratitude-filled.

I am repeatedly reminded when I step out of balance, that balance is a skill set, it is dynamic, and recoverable. If I shift my focus from being right to being effective, I become more compassionate with myself and others. It doesn't really matter, in this moment, how many people I seek to assist. The real question is, how many can I assist with the resources I have? Assisting more, giving back more, doing more, now means getting more resources, rather than throwing myself out of balance.

Unleash Your Goddess

Now that I am sustainably running a seven figure company, the same truths stand; time, energy and money have to be measured and managed to provide the balance that I call success. I can tell you that the lessons of self-first are firmly and gratefully ingrained in me, and when I do need to over-extend, it is for a short while only, and my tribe helps to pull me back into line. After all, there are seven billion people out there. They are always going to need more than you alone can provide for, or source.

The way to successfully build yourself up is from the inside out. Organic truth, authenticity, service and gratitude are necessary foundations if you seek to be unapologetically yourself. Delve deep within, be the magnificent being you are and *Unleash Your Inner Goddess*, she is waiting for you.

The Goddess doesn't enter us from outside;
she emerges from deep within.
She is not held back by what happened in the past.
She is conceived in consciousness, born in love,
and nurtured by higher thinking.
She is integrity and value, created and
sustained by the hard work of personal growth
and the discipline of a life lived actively in hope.

Marianne Williamson

Michele Maher

Michele Maher is a published author, and a certified Kundalini Reiki Master. She is a true creative leader, empowering women in her FemCity Collective group, a renowned jewelry designer with Michele Maher Designs and Founder of Pivot with Positivity. Michele believes that women have been told for far too long what they should or shouldn't wear, what they should look like, and what they should or shouldn't do, say and be. She lives her truth and is unapologetically herself. Michele is a cat lover, and lives with her husband and two children in Toronto, Canada.

The Maverick Mindset

Michele Maher

Great things are not accomplished
by those that yield to trends
and fads and popular opinion.

Jack Kerouac

Coming Into My Own

As a child, I was raised to follow the rules, to do what was expected of me and not to make waves. Other than a few *"pushing the envelope"* moments—like four-year-old me painting my nails in kindergarten class while the teacher was talking—I always listened and did as I was told. If my mom told me to sit still and play with my toys, I did so; I didn't move from that spot. That *doing as I was told and expected of me* behavior and people pleasing continued throughout much of my life. However, it never quite felt like me *inside*.

I was a born leader and entrepreneur, yet I never realized it, or rather, I didn't actually do anything with it until much later in my life. I believe I always had it inside of me, but let's just say, it was never encouraged for me to nurture that part of myself. It has been a true journey of finding my way while doing things much differently from everyone else.

I have always been a creative, out-of-the-box thinker but I wasn't able to express it to its fullest. Sure, there were glimpses of it here and there, but for the most part, I had *"played it safe"* and always did what was expected of me. While some people are confident and show the world what *"they got,"* others suppress their uniqueness, hide in their box so that nobody sees it. They conform to society, never truly showing the world who they are. Well, that was me from childhood to late adulthood. I was *"in the box"* by conforming, people pleasing, feeling unworthy and stifled. I wanted to be freer, to get out of the box, but didn't know how to.

The Catalyst

As a child I never liked to follow the crowd. This was even more apparent in high school. I totally hated it there and could not wait until it was over. I never once fit in. I went to class and got out of there as soon as I could every day.

The school uniform made my high school experience even worse. To me, there was nothing nice about any of it. It was ugly as hell—a yucky-brown polyester blazer, yellow blouse, and a kilt that was green and brown plaid. Plus, I didn't like looking like everyone else, and so, in my quest to continue to be different while expressing my individuality, I proceeded to load on the jewelry. This was a time when punk rock and goth were gaining ground, so I hung out with some of the kids who were also taking the uniform to another level. Needless to say, I wasn't hanging out with the popular kids.

On one of my many trips shopping downtown which I loved to do, I found myself at a bead store which turned out to be a life-changing event. I decided to pick up some supplies to start playing with the idea of designing my own jewelry to wear. This was something that called to me and made my heart sing. I also enjoyed sewing and designing Barbie clothes. I had so many ideas in my head and so many designs. I used to draw them out on my doodle pads. Designing things ignited a passion in me. It was my way to express my uniqueness and show the *real me* to the world. *I was ready.*

It was at this time that I decided to tell my parents that I wanted to enroll at Ontario College of Art and Design and take Fashion Design. My parents' reaction was not what I expected: *"You don't want to end up as a starving artist," "You'll never make money that way," "You will be poor forever," "You're good at math, you need to go to university and become an accountant, that is what you need to do."* I couldn't help thinking, Whoa! What? But I didn't rebel. I went to University and took a Bachelor of Commerce with Economics, with a Minor in Psychology.

Messages From The Universe

I ended up becoming an accountant, specializing in complex audits. First, I worked in a chartered accountancy firm, then for the government supporting the trading floor, and finally, I was working at a major bank. These were demanding roles in what I felt were stifling corporate environments. Did I love the work?

Yes. I loved the people, I loved most of the work, but I never felt like I belonged. I continued my passion for jewelry and wore pieces that expressed my uniqueness; however, in each position, upper management looked at me like I had two heads most of the time. It wasn't the norm that an accountant would wear bold jewelry. I pushed so many buttons and norms at each place I worked, questioning why things were done the way they were. The standard answer: *"Because it has always been done this way."*

You know how the Universe always sends us messages to steer us towards our path? Well, I have had many of those. I had experienced being laid off at two previous accountancy firms which made me feel like a failure. However, I didn't expect that after twelve years at the bank, that out of the blue, I would be let go. I was given a package and sent home in a cab—not allowed to go back to my desk or talk to anyone. I was in total shock. The Universe decided it was time to knock me in the head again, this time with enough force that I got the message.

Talk about feeling unworthy? I had spent most of my life trying to prove myself to others, doing what my parents wanted, what society expected of me, and trying to fit into the box. I was never accepted. I felt that I had failed again.

I almost ignored the message from the Universe again. As part of my package, I was given a thirty-day period to find a new job within the bank and I spent my time applying. Thankfully that went nowhere, and the time passed without my finding another job. One day during that summer (which I took off to be with my kids) I realized that I had been given a gift; that I could finally follow that passion I had long lost. I picked up jewelry supplies and started creating—this time, not just for myself and my family, but rather to start selling. That September I scheduled an Open House at my home and started creating! *Wow…* it was a success and everyone loved my designs. I was told how talented I was over and over again.

Mindset Makeover

Throughout my entrepreneurial journey, there have been many lessons that have been part of my evolution to embrace myself as a leader and a businesswoman. Much of this wisdom has resulted in my mindset makeover. These are 5 pivotal lessons I have learned:

LESSON 1:

Don't rush to the first person you meet who promises you "a six-figure income in six-months."

Why resist temptation?
There will always be more.

Don Herold

Let me tell you about my first outing ever as an entrepreneur—keep in mind I had never before networked and even at corporate events I wouldn't speak to anyone I didn't know. I sat down beside a business coach not knowing one iota about running a business. I think she could smell my naiveté from a mile away. Needless to say, she convinced me that I needed her services at a price I could not afford, and I signed up for a year.

I learned a lot from this coach, but even still, when I cancelled after a year, I went on to find other coaches, kind of running around trying them out to find the right fit. Let me tell you one thing: take the time to feel out any coaches or mentors etc., as there are so many out there. Because of my past feelings of being unworthy and not good enough, I got sucked in by many who played on that. I realize now that this was all part of my journey of finding my own way, the courage to stand on my own, to speak up and declare that I am indeed worthy, and that I am enough.

LESSON 2:

You need to be open to new things.

> *Every new experience brings its own*
> *maturity and a greater clarity of vision.*
>
> **Indira Gandhi**

I never did any personal development work in my twenty years working in corporate environments, but in the seven years I have been an entrepreneur, I have definitely made up for it! It's like a light switch went on and I had the drive to learn. I could see the potential, I could see what I could become, and I could see that saying *your thoughts become things* is so true! It's not like I woke up one morning, went to a conference and all of the sudden I got it, and was transformed. No, it doesn't happen like that: you go to a conference, hear the speakers, some pieces resonate. You think, *"Wow I am totally pumped,"* then you go home and get back into your routine and what you heard is forgotten. Then you do it again, and again, and again, and each time you remember a little more, you make that tiny little change, you catch yourself in the moment and you think, *"What did I learn again?"* And that behavior gets modified.

It's all baby steps, but as we all know, a series of little baby steps can translate to some significant changes over time. It's all about persistence, and surrounding yourself with the right people, the ones who will push you, and who will see that glory inside of you, and who will keep cheering you on. Let me tell you though: the hardest part of being an entrepreneur and keeping your head up and continuing to move forward is controlling that little voice in your head which tells you it can't be done, or questions you, continually asking you *"Who do you think you are?" "Why do you think you can do that?" "You've never done that before."*

I think that little voice has stopped so many of us, especially women, and held us back from speaking our truth, standing out and holding firm on how we truly feel. Let me talk about the partner to that little voice—judgment—and the fear it holds over us. It is that inner voice of judgment that asks, *"What will people think of me, what will people say?"*

This is another dream killer. Unfortunately people will judge, and there is nothing we can do about it. However, it is crucial to know that the people who judge you, the things they say and do, have nothing, and I mean *nothing*, to do with you. They are projecting their own fears and worries onto you. There is a famous quote which I have seen go around and around and it always hits me as being one of the best, *"What people think of me is none of my business."*

To be able to take this to heart is not easy, nor is it instant. For me, this has been another part of my journey, moving from being an accountant to following my passion has led to a lot of judgment from family and friends. I remember going places and people would say, *"Have you found a job yet or are you still doing that jewelry thing?"*

What the %$#? That would trigger the anger in me like you would not believe. Again, this has been a work in progress, but I can tell you if someone does say that to me now, I am no longer speechless.

LESSON 3:

There is no such thing as, *"I am just a…"* You can be all that and more!

> *All the power is within you.*
> *You can do anything.*
>
> **Swami Vivekananda**

Being an entrepreneur is all about being a *"jack of all trades."* However, I do remember early on in my entrepreneurial journey being told *"You don't want to do more than one thing or you will confuse people."* This was said to me when I decided to join an MLM (Multi-Level Marketing) company which at the time, offered a natural hair care product line. I was severely criticized for working on more than one business at a time. Many people told me I had to have only one so-called *"what I do"* or potential customers would be unsure and not buy from me at all.

Well, I have learned many lessons since that time, and it really is about being of *service to people.* You never really are selling a product; if someone wants an item, chances are they have many avenues to purchase it. People buy from you, or deal with you through your services, because it is *you*. As you develop and hone your own skills, remembering that we are all here to help and to serve each other, you will attract those people who like and trust you. These are the people you will do business with. The products are a means to an end. In my case, the products and services I offer are all about making women look and feel amazing, confident, and authentic. Clients come to me because they want to align with me. It is because of our connection that they are willing to buy my products and services.

LESSON 4:

Don't be afraid to put yourself out there. Nike's *"Just Do It"* is my favorite slogan of all time.

Be yourself; everyone else is already taken.

Oscar Wilde

I would have to say my biggest transformation came in the last two years, when the COVID-19 pandemic was declared and the world shut down. I had a moment of extreme fear, as I watched the news and heard that sports and Las Vegas were shutting down. That felt like the end of the world to me. I just wanted to crawl into my bed and hide.

That was Friday, March 13th. On Sunday March 15th I had an epiphany in the shower. I realized that I knew so many people with a voice and many of them were ready to share it with the world and speak their truth. All they needed was a boost, some encouragement, and they would do it. So on Monday morning I was reaching out to my contacts asking them to come on video with me to talk about what we were going through. The aim was to help others who were struggling to see the possibilities and the positive side of things. That is how my podcast *"Pivot with Positivity"* was born!

In 2020, I completed over one hundred interviews on YouTube and decided to also start a group on Facebook where I would share only positivity and uplifting posts along with the interviews. Stepping into action is what saved me from falling into the black hole of fear, plus the conversations I had with the most amazing people in my network—the amount of personal and spiritual growth I experienced that year was incredible!

That's my advice to you: *action* is the one thing that will move you out of a situation fast, and like the saying goes, *"Jump and the net will appear."* This was another example of learning to use my voice, and to provide a voice for others. Let me tell you, just as everything always is, it was never as scary as I had made it out to be in my head.

LESSON 5:

You always have to be ready to pivot.

> *Pivoting isn't plan B;*
> *It's part of the process.*
>
> **Jeff Goins**

I think this lesson is not even limited to entrepreneurs. This lesson stretches into each and every person involved in this thing called *"life."* If we have learned anything from this pandemic, it is exactly this: you need to be able to turn on a dime, to shift your focus, attention, and resources, *just like that*. Entrepreneurs do have an advantage here as they always need to be pivoting, shifting, learning, and growing. I am on a healing and a spiritual path, which intensified during the latter half of 2021. At that time, I was healing my inner child, tuning into my intuition, focusing on the power of energy, and was working on even more modalities of self-healing. This began in 2020 with my Level I Reiki training and continued as I embraced the true power of crystals and energy healing. I brought all of this into my jewelry designs. So much of what we are taught and brought up believing, especially in society and projected by the media, is just not true. Everything is energy, and our power to create our own reality is one hundred percent accurate. We are not finite beings. Our potential has not even been close to becoming fully realized. Every day we hear stories of records broken in the sports world, illnesses healed, personal feats accomplished, etc. We are only limited by our minds and our unconscious programming.

It is time for us all to throw that out the window and reach for our dreams. It is crucial that we step out of our comfort zone and forget what society, parents, and family have told us. It is time to speak our truth and stand out in the world with no regrets. We all have a message to share with the world, and we never know who we are going to inspire doing so. I have so many people reaching out to me now thanking me for sharing the truth, for continuing to speak my mind, and telling me how this has inspired them to use their voice and to speak up despite the fear of being judged. It is just like any muscle, it takes time to build it, but it becomes stronger and stronger. The sad truth about all of this *leveling up* though is that you are going to leave others behind. Some people are meant to only be in your life for a short time and others longer. The stagnant ones go, and you find new ones along the way.

Embrace Yourself

This is all part of life. For me, the journey has been one of finding my tribe, of discovering where I belong. Fully recognizing who I am, believing in myself, and shifting my Maverick Mindset has been an evolution. I have given myself the permission to continue to grow spiritually. Never would I have imagined myself becoming a Kundalini Reiki Master, infusing the healing powers of the crystals into my jewelry designs, and going on to healing others. I feel like I am on the right path and finally becoming my authentic self in this unending journey of life. Life is short and there is only one you. Love yourself unapologetically and don't wait another second to embrace all that is beautiful in all of you—mind, body, and soul.

Beauty begins the moment you decide to be yourself.

Coco Chanel

Never retract, never explain, never apologize.
Just get things done and let them howl.

Nellie McClung

Mali Phonpadith

Mali Phonpadith is the Founder/CEO of SOAR Community Network and Co-Founder of SOAR Nebula, a global resource hub for transcendent leaders. She is a TEDx Speaker, multi-published International Bestselling Author, Certified Talent Optimization Leader and Diversity, Equity and Inclusion consultant, leadership development trainer and facilitator. Her firm, SOAR, helps organizational leaders map strategic priorities and build C3 cultures where Compassionate leaders thrive, Cohesive teams drive results and employees Collaborate and innovate.

Refugee To Soarpreneur

Mali Phonpadith

*Whoever renders service to many, puts himself
in line for greatness — great wealth, great return,
great satisfaction, great reputation, and great joy.*

Jim Rohn

Beneath the surface of its natural beauty and the proud people
of Laos, the country of my birth, is a history of trauma, grief,
unhealed wounds and hidden landmines. In 1975, the Vietnam
War had been officially declared over but it still raged in Laos.
My family lived in the upper half of the panhandle where so
much devastation was spread, with the Vietnam border to its
east. The North Vietnamese army had established the infamous
Ho Chi Minh Trail as a route for supplies and troops. This caused
the sky to rain bombs.

At the tender age of four years old, half asleep, in the dark of
night, my family fled our homeland, Laos on a tiny boat as we
made our way to a refugee camp in Thailand. Escaping with only
the moonlight, we made it across the Mekong River. We arrived

to the shore—the exact coordinates that my father had spent years mapping out. Relatives who were living in Thailand met us and hid us in a produce truck, stacking boxes of vegetables to hide us. When we reached a *'safe house,'* we stayed with these relatives for a couple of weeks while my father and relatives mapped out a way to get us inside a nearby, overcrowded refugee camp.

Brave New World

One year later, in 1980, a church in Maryland sponsored us and we were able to become permanent residents of the United States. Our first place of residence was in Washington, D.C., which at that time was considered the murder capital of the U.S. My grandmother said we exchanged bombs for bullets.

Once we landed in the States, members of the church helped us rent an apartment. My father was able to find work at a nearby car dealership. Since he did not speak English, the only job he qualified for was a janitor position. He was ecstatic to have work, the opportunity to earn money and support his family. While he appreciated the immense generosity we had experienced from the church members, my father worked hard to reclaim his sense of independence. He wanted to earn his own way and no longer wished to rely on the church or government food stamps.

Our family lived in a small one bedroom apartment with broken windows during that first long winter filled with freezing temperatures. Each room housed one family, all refugees, who had escaped the aftermath of the Vietnam War. Imagine, sharing one bedroom with seven people and very little money for food and clothing. We certainly were not living a calm, harmonious or stress free lifestyle. This new world we entered may not have been war torn, but from the sounds of sirens, bullets, and growls from empty stomachs, it was going to be full of battles.

Clarity Of Purpose

I knew even as a child, that I had to prepare for a very rough societal climb in order to get to a place of safety and financial security for my family. That inner knowing evoked an emotional commitment to design a life that would lead my family out of poverty. When, how and through what means, I had no clue. I was only seven years old when I made this commitment to myself and for my family. The one thing that I did know was that I would one day own my own business. In my mind, that meant I would be able to design my own financial freedom. That was my definition of success.

How do these early childhood experiences impact a child's life trajectory? Well, the little girl living within me became extremely driven. I moved forward in life as if I were the adult and my parents were my children. My mother and father never officially asked me to play this role as their executor or guardian. I took it upon myself and didn't complain. I focused on the end goal, which was living a life where we no longer had to walk long distances to the grocery stores and pay the cashier with government subsidized food stamps.

My father was determined for us to become self-sufficient as quickly as possible. I learned a lot from him while he was still alive. I watched how hard he worked and how little he complained. I guess he felt lucky to be alive considering he had been captured and sent to the re-education camp while we were still living in Laos. He was forced to do hard labor and witnessed many of his friends and peers die during that dark time in his life. My father worried a lot but mostly silently.

When I was seven or eight years old, I wrote out the checks to help my parents cover our bills. At that time, I had already gone to school and learned English and Math. Prior to that, members of the church who sponsored us, volunteered to help us wherever they could. Once my siblings and I were old enough and able to take on these responsibilities, naturally, we did so as if it was designed by nature and not by our circumstances. We simply did what we had to do and naively thought that every child had these same roles and responsibilities to fulfill for the benefit of the family.

You Can Do Hard Things

If you want something you've never had,
you've got to do something you've never done.

Thomas Edison

After a couple of years living in Washington, D.C., our church was able to help us rent an apartment in Maryland. Both my father and mother tried to go to night school and learn English through programs designed for newly arrived refugees. Unfortunately, with a family of seven, they could barely make ends meet and eventually my mother went to work as a hotel housekeeper where she worked for over thirty years before retiring. My father, at that time, worked

Mondays through Saturdays as a janitor at two car dealerships, working morning until night. On Sundays he would often contact church members to see about painting their fences, mowing their lawns, and doing any odd job possible to earn additional income. It was through my parents' hard work, persistence and determination that in 1987, seven years after we landed in the United States, even with their minimum wage jobs and lack of English proficiency, put a down payment of $20,000 in cash to buy our first single family home. We grew up with very little and yet we never felt poor. My grandmother, father and mother, through their actions, showed us how to accomplish the impossible. Owning their home was symbolic. They were able to build a loving home in a new land while living with the permanent wounds of war.

My parents never set out to be role models. They just did what they needed to do. In turn, by watching them strive to be better for themselves and us as a family, they shaped me in my formative years into becoming who I am today. They demonstrated that all is possible when it came to work ethic, setting specific goals with intentions and manifesting our desired outcomes into reality and that we shouldn't shy away from hard things. I watched them accomplish what others in similar situations may have never allowed themselves to imagine possible. I watched and I took it all in. I noticed how they were able to accomplish so much, quietly, persistently, and courageously.

Through them, I learned how to work hard and do whatever it took to accomplish what my mind set out to do. With these lessons I was able to graduate high school at the top of my class. I worked part-time starting at the age of fifteen to help my parents with the bills and committed all my other waking hours to my studies, knowing that scholarships were going to be required if I wanted to attend college. I was awarded a few thousand dollars to help cover my first year of tuition at university. After the first two semesters, I worked full-time so that I could pay for the remaining years to graduation.

In the end, the hard work with very little sleep paid off and I graduated in five years, magna cum laude, with degrees in International Business, Marketing and Spanish. Lessons from my childhood taught me that if I was going to accomplish anything and be successful, I needed to work hard physically, develop my skills and talents mentally, and push my emotions aside to focus on the goals I needed to accomplish.

Success, as I understood it, was an external place or thing to *"get to."* I didn't realize, until much later, when I launched my own business, that success also includes feelings, emotions, sense of harmony, passion and satisfaction. I learned then, that if I wanted to reach my goals, I had to set intentions and take the daily steps necessary to manifest them into reality.

Tragedy Strikes

Two months after college graduation, I was hired by a government contractor to join their commercial marketing division. At age twenty-two, I was responsible for submitting a marketing plan to the Vice President for consideration. In preparation for this project, I was introduced to a gentleman named Chris, who was part of the federal marketing team. I shared an office with him and he became my friend and mentor. After working closely together for months on end, our friendship blossomed into admiration, which then turned into love. Five years flew by and he proposed marriage.

As life creates its twists and turns throughout our journeys, my path came to a halt when I was twenty-seven years old. On a hot summer day in 2003, Chris and I went on a family picnic. I was excited to introduce him to my extended family and friends as my new fiancé. It was during this picnic that my world as I knew it, stopped.

As I was finishing up with food preparations, I walked toward the water to see that Chris and my brother-in-law were waist high in the Potomac River, talking and laughing while our nephews and relatives were splashing water at each other. Within seconds, Chris must have felt my presence from afar because he turned around and waved at me. He motioned for me to join them but I held up five fingers, as I still needed a few minutes to finish up with the food prep. He nodded as if to say, *"Ok"* and gave me a thumbs up signal. I smiled, waved and made my way toward the picnic tables. That was the last gesture he ever offered me.

Soon after I walked away from the scene, there was a riptide that came in and swept away five of the boys who were wading in the water. My brother-in-law and Chris swam out to rescue them. They were able to bring four to safety with help from nearby jet skiers. Unfortunately, Chris lost his life trying to save the last child, my brother-in-law's nephew, and they both left this earthly plane together that afternoon.

Witnessing all of this taking place right before my eyes, my mind and body tried to protect me. They shut down and I passed out. When I woke up, I remember wearing an oxygen mask inside one of the ambulances that was part of the search and rescue team. There are no words to describe what the body and the spirit go through when everything about your existence and your physical and emotional capacity gets completely flipped upside down. It felt like a truck hit my entire being and shattered me into thousands of pieces. It would take years to find the energy and will to gather and piece together all the broken parts so that I could feel like myself again. The truth is, even with all the pieces newly intact, I would be forever changed by that devastating loss.

Finding Purpose In Service

It was at least eight months before I could see or think straight and another year before I fully reached acceptance that my journey had taken a different course than the one I had planned. Coming to terms with this reality created a fresh starting point. As I embarked on creating a new beginning, it included a change in my career.

By January of 2004, I decided to leave my job and start a financial practice where I could turn my sadness into service. I grew my practice by speaking to groups about the importance of planning, at a young age, even before marriage, so that the financial struggles I had faced after my fiancé passed away would not be something my clients ever experienced in their own lives. I was so passionate about sharing my story to help others that I found myself working extremely long hours, traveling up and down the highway to meet as many people as I could. I used work as my vehicle to get back the hope I had lost and do the healing that I so much desired.

But that is where my old fears began hijacking my brain. Old beliefs and habits about doing whatever it takes and getting to success at whatever cost, took over my mind and body without me even realizing it. This time, success to me was not about moving away from poverty. It was about feeling again and activating my heart. My work of helping others and protecting them from what I went through became the drug that made me feel alive again. Quite frankly, I became a workaholic. I found myself getting up at 5:00 am working and writing until 2:00 am, making this a new pattern. I didn't want to go to sleep because I didn't want to experience any more nightmares. It was better to stay awake, to experience life and be with the light of the world. I wasn't interested in shutting my eyes and experiencing any more darkness, even if that meant sacrificing my rest.

Of course, at the time, I didn't realize that these habits formed to protect me from additional pain. This also validated what I learned as a child. When you want something, work hard and do whatever it takes to get to where you want to go. Where I wanted to go was *any* place that didn't feel sad and lonely. I found every opportunity and reason to see people, share my insights, and inspire them to protect their loved ones through insurance and investing in their financial future. My work offered that warm security blanket and I liked it that way.

Pushing The Comfort Zone

At my first networking event after launching the practice, I remember feeling nervous and very much alone. There was a moment when I thought to myself, *"What am I doing? I have no idea how to run a business. Is building this practice even going to work?"* I thought about leaving the networking event and just go home, curl up in my bed and cry. But then I heard another voice in my head say; *"You have no other choice but to move on with your life. He cannot come back and the only place for you to turn is forward."* I took in a deep breath, drew out a sigh and pushed myself to stay and rallied my inner thoughts to focus. I challenged myself to find the first friendly face that walked through the door and forced myself to stay.

Several people walked in and then I spotted a man who entered the room with a smile. I remember looking down at his hand and when I spotted a wedding ring, I was certain he was the one to approach. It was safe. He was married and there would be no room for misunderstanding. I went for it. I walked up to him, learned that his name was Victor, and told him that this was my first time at this networking event. He mentioned that it was his first time as well. We navigated the room together that morning and agreed to stay in touch. He and his wife became clients of mine. As the years went by, we met twice a year for seven years to discuss his financial goals. We became good friends, like so many of my other clients. Victor, however, would become more than a friend. He became *(and perhaps always was)* my soul mate.

Within a nine-year timeframe, I also experienced the losses of my father, godfather and uncle, all to cancer. I grieved the loss of my best friend, who left this earth by way of suicide and said goodbye to my grandmother who I adored.

During this same tumultuous yet liberating time, Victor, yes, the man I met eight months after losing Chris, called me to share that he had separated from his wife. We became friends and our feelings for one another grew. Neither of us truly knew when it had turned from friendship into love. It slowly happened and it blossomed through our shared values and vision for life.

As complex as it was, both understanding that he was still in the midst of a separation, there was a knowing that we would be fine regardless of what direction our friendship needed to take. We both agreed that peace had to be a part of the equation.

It took several years before I could tap into a *"lightness of being,"* which I had never experienced before, not even as a child. It was only then, when my spirit felt more awake and free; where I was able to make decisions based on love, hope and abundance versus lack and scarcity. When this moment of clarity arrived, I knew that it would take daily practice to stay calm on a consistent basis. I was thirty-six years old when I was finally able to tap into these feelings and live with trust and faith that, *"all is as it should be, or it would be something else."*

As fate would painfully have it, the same week that Victor and his wife submitted their divorce papers, she was diagnosed with leukemia. Within eight months she passed away peacefully with her loved ones, including Victor, by her side.

Life offers so many contradictions including pain and joy, hatred and love, light and dark, life and death. I have come to learn that our life experiences, especially the most painful ones, create an empathy bucket that stretches far and wide. Because I truly understood what happens to a human heart when you lose someone you love, I was able to support Victor on his personal journey of loss and healing. It made us grow closer. This new, yet unwanted experience, bonded and solidified our friendship. Today he is my best friend, husband, business partner, and life companion.

Wellness Is The New Rich

Wealth is the ability to fully experience life.

Henry David Thoreau

After experiencing so much on my journey, I have come to realize that the key *for living a rich life* is about being intentional and using all the tools necessary on a daily basis. It is to ensure that I am creating my own inner calm and not allowing fear to dictate how I operate. This realization has taken me years to rewire and shift old habits and unhealthy patterns of behaviors. During my childhood to age thirty-five, I couldn't recall ever *feeling like a child*. I only remember participating in life with an adult's mind. I was in my mid-thirties when I had this inspiration. It was one of the defining moments for me. I asked myself, *"What would life look like if I made decisions based on abundance and trust versus with a lack mindset and fear?"* That's when I began my personal development journey. I read books, signed up for retreats, traveled to expose myself to new insights and wisdom.

I began to play and explore life with a childlike approach. I wanted to experience the world with the most innocent, pure eyes, heart and mind. I desired to be free from the heaviness of my own expectations, fear based roles and responsibilities I created for myself. I wanted to rid my worries of not having enough. Attaining wellness, harmony, and peace was *now* going to be my measure of success.

Soarpeneur

I mentioned that I uncovered a feeling of lightness at the age of thirty-six. That year, 2011, with the advice of my managing partner and peers, I left my financial practice and decided to launch my own company to help small and midsize businesses develop compassionate, transcendent leaders to drive their missions forward. The company has grown into what is now the SOAR Community Network. I realized that so many people don't give themselves permission to soar, to be happy, to heal and move forward. SOAR is an acronym: we want organizational leaders to *See, Own, Articulate and Release* their unique message and mission into the world through conscious leadership.

Today, I run a successful and thriving company from a place of peace and service. The company has grown with the help of a very supportive husband/business partner, through our acquisition of another organizational development firm and support from a community of extraordinary souls. Our work holds me accountable and reminds me of my new definition of success. I am much more capable of catching myself before repeating old habits and changing the internal dialogue whenever necessary to ensure I'm honoring the path to a healthier, holistic version of success. I don't work with that anxiety sitting inside my chest anymore and I can sleep through the night now. The lightness within my being provides me with a freedom that I've never known before. This sense of well-being confirms that my success in this lifetime has finally arrived. The rest is about continuous learning, personal growth and helping others do the same.

Our overall wellness and designing our lives to make room for harmony and happiness is a moment-by-moment, conscious, decision-making process. Our desired outcome, mine being wellness as my new definition of success, can only be attained when we're intentional about creating a life with more peace than anxiety. This is where mindfulness practices such as meditation, EFT, energy medicine and all other healing modalities come in.

As a *Soarpreneur*, I am constantly and consciously shifting my energy between my soul's desire to fully exist, make a difference with passion and purpose and my human need to feel safe along the journey. This is ever evolving and a work in progress. Creating a healthy and happy lifestyle while building a business comes with its challenges but knowing when my internal (harmony) compass needs calibration is essential. Listening to our bodies, learning how to protect and replenish our energy, and taking time to rest the spirit, are all practices I have implemented and teach others to do in their lives and businesses.

Old habits are not easy to break, however, with enough commitment, practice and purpose driven action, we can shift our old belief systems. We have to serve our higher selves by living our life by design through our conscious awareness. Our higher self knows the way to live a life of peace, service and purposeful mission. Your definitions of success and abundance are as individual as you are. Give yourself permission to evolve, define your own success and SOAR.

When you are able to shift your inner awareness
to how you can serve others, and when you make this the
central focus of your life, you will then be in a position
to know true miracles in your progress toward prosperity.

Wayne W. Dyer

In order to kick ass,
you must first lift up your foot.

Jen Sincero

Anna Zeccolo Reeves

Anna Zeccolo Reeves, is a published author and passionate Soulpreneur. She is a Certified Master NLP Coach and RTT Practitioner. Anna is a coach at Anna Z Coaching, the Founder/CEO of Tiny Chefs Inc., and the Tiny Chefs Franchise. Her passion is to provide women an opportunity to gain greater clarity around their relationships with themselves and others. A single mother of 3 girls, she currently resides in Maryland with them and her Shih Tzu, Bella.

Ignite Your Power Within

Anna Zeccolo Reeves

*The most common way people give up their power
is by thinking they don't have any.*

Alice Walker

I was an only child for the first eight years of my life. My parents
married when I was a baby and divorced when I was two. Growing
up with my mom as the sole caregiver provided me with lots of
opportunities for one-to-one time with her. The love and connection were strong and steady, and it provided me with a warm blanket
of security. I always knew my mom loved me.

Being her dependent meant she had to go to work for the two
of us. There were many babysitters and a lot of alone time. So much
so, that I grew up playing alone, in my room mainly, but also in the
yard, or at the babysitter. All the while, my mom handled our home
life and her work schedule. I believe spending a lot of time alone
during my formative years had a lot to do with how I came into my
journey as an entrepreneur.

I was a quiet child, always choosing to do the right thing, whatever that thing was. I didn't want to let the adults around me down. I just wanted to be the child I was expected to be. Not only was I the oldest in my family, but I was also the first grandchild on both sides. My grandmother on my mom's side treated me especially well because I was a girl and she had raised seven children, all boys with exception to my mom. Love and attention were poured all over me, so I felt special.

Disconnected

However, I had a less than ideal relationship with my father. My parents were so young when they got pregnant with me, and the stresses of a baby mixed with being a first-born girl in an Italian family, created a bit of a divide between him and I. It was never explicitly said to me, but there was always the underlying feeling of not being wanted. I played this feeling down as I grew, but nonetheless it existed, it haunted my understanding of my history. I suspect my desire to be good, quiet, and easy, played into my psyche, because as I grew, so did my desire to please people.

I never felt good enough around my father. I knew I was appreciated by my mother but as my brother, sister, and stepbrother came along, I faded into the background because I chose to be the *"easy one."* I never asked for what I wanted in terms of attention from either parent because I knew they were doing the best they could with the resources they had. I didn't want to impose or add more stress, so I kept quiet and to myself.

I also never felt good enough in social settings. At the time, I couldn't pinpoint why I felt I didn't fit in, although now as an adult I can reflect and see that it was my inner child not being connected to myself. My inner girl-child didn't have a secure attachment to her father. I was the good girl seeking external approval for attention from her mother. This *outside seeking* left me feeling depleted and at a loss for self-love.

What I have learned is that no matter what events occurred, it was me who created meaning out of such events. When you see through the lens of your reality, you can only see it this way. You can live a lifetime holding onto feelings that aren't even real, but nonetheless they guide you in how you show up in life. I was living what I thought was a meaningless life when in fact I had everything I needed in life to succeed. I just needed a road map, a way to tap into my internal guide.

Poverty

Growing up poor set me apart from my classmates and taught me to not ask for things I wanted. The financial and emotional stress in the house I grew up in sat heavy in the air like smoke in a burning house. It was so prevalent that no one dared whine for toys or clothes or extras because food and utilities were first. *"Money didn't grow on trees"* was a popular mantra when we did ask for more. My mom repeatedly told me that I would be the child in the family going to college because she had it in the divorce agreement that my father was to pay for it. This was ingrained in me so I had hope in the future that I could somehow get out of the poverty that I knew too well.

There wasn't much in the way of confidence being modeled to me as a child either. No fault of anyone, it's just a fact. This was a driver into my *"playing small"* as I grew up, and I felt I wasn't equipped to play the game of life as well as most of my peers. I went for the career of elementary school teacher mainly because I loved kids, but also because I just wasn't privy to other types of careers. There was a special place in my heart for kids, especially vulnerable kids from the wrong side of the tracks or from poor families. Something about these kids felt familiar to me. I pursued a teaching career, but deep down I wanted to be a psychologist. I wanted to study people and why they did what they did. I convinced myself that I didn't have the *"book smarts"* or the resilience for all that schooling. It's funny how things worked out because in my thirties I created a kids cooking company called Tiny Chefs, and in my forties, I created a coaching company focused on women's empowerment. I had the smarts and resilience all along, but not the belief.

Soul Purpose

As a child, one of the many things I did to prevent boredom at home was to bake. Ingredients didn't cost too much so I made cookies, bars, doughs, and whatever else using any ingredients I could get my hands on. It felt so empowering and freeing to experiment on my own and to create delicious treats for the entire family to enjoy. I received a lot of praise and rarely made mistakes. This is where I felt the most confident in my world. I always thought it would be fun to be a pastry chef.

Teaching will always be a quality that connects me to others, whether it be kids or adults, working with food, or working with people on their mindset. Creating two small businesses and a third company for the purpose of franchising, Tiny Chefs came with many ups and downs. In my twenties I taught kids how to read and write and associate school and learning to have fun. In my thirties, I built onto this, with teaching kids how to work with food, and challenge themselves to do unfamiliar things. In my forties I created the Tiny Chefs Franchise Company for the sole purpose of teaching women how to start and run their own Tiny Chefs business. I believe in the power of systems to provide structure, consistency, and growth. Additionally, my coaching company, Anna Z Coaching, teaches women how to connect with their divine feminine power.

F*ck Fear

Let fear be a counselor and not a jailer.

Tony Robbins

Fear seemed to have always been with me from a very young age. I feared making people angry, feared making conversations with new people, feared not making good enough grades, and feared using my voice to expose truths. While I used fear to keep me safe growing up, during the making of Tiny Chefs I used fear to drive me towards my goals. As I founded Tiny Chefs, I truly believed that the concept of a turnkey program and at home cooking parties and events would be a success, even though no other company in the area was offering anything like it. I had many supporters and a few others along the way looked at me as if I was crazy and didn't support me.

As Tiny Chefs grew and grew, not only did I believe more than ever that my concept could be an excellent way to reach kids differently, but I also began to realize that whatever I thought in my head could manifest in reality. There was a sense of security and comfort that while I didn't know a thing about running a small business, I could figure it out on my own. Here is where I am thankful for those years I spent alone in my childhood. There was an ease about me that I didn't need anyone else to help me get ahead. In retrospect, I now know that I would have made faster progress if I had a network to assist me, but you live and learn.

Tiny Chefs

Four years into the making of Tiny Chefs, I was informed by my then-husband that by the end of that year, my business needed to generate enough profit to withdraw a small amount for the family or else it would be considered a hobby. This was my first wake-up call, and I took it seriously. I decided right then and there to *"turn it up"* so that I could grow this toddler company into adolescence. I had to fight my natural *"I'm not good enough"* instincts and to do uncomfortable tasks, such being featured on the news to gain awareness, and I had to commit to learning about components of running a business that I feared so much: leading people, marketing, sales, and the forbidden finance.

I was naturally good at working with kids and food, but it is everything outside of these that eventually gave me the grit I possess today when it comes to leading my companies. Tiny Chefs gave me the opportunity to discover ways to go outside my comfort zone. I learned how to stand up for what I needed to make the company grow and prosper, and this alone stopped me from the people-pleasing that plagued my life.

I had to say *"no"* to certain hosting partnerships as the benefits didn't outweigh the challenges of working with difficult companies. I developed a keen eye for what was in the best interest of the company and could make tough decisions simply by following my gut instinct. If I wanted to grow, I also needed to give up the reins of the company beginning with hiring staff to support me in the field.

My first dabble with this was when I hired staff to work on the actual parties with me. I remember the first person I interviewed told me in the meeting that she wanted to work with me so that she could learn how it was done and then start her own cooking company. Ridiculous as it sounds, it helped me to realize that I needed to ask my lawyer to create a non-compete agreement to protect me.

Playing Small

I'll admit, that until recently, I still played small and struggled with exercising my authentic voice. This came in the form of allowing Directors to veer off from my lead and me not wanting to rock the boat, in my own company. Part of my staying quiet was my underlying belief that standing up for myself meant that I wouldn't be liked. Another part was that I didn't want to believe it was true that I was being taken advantage of.

Two of the former Directors did run off and work with our hosting partners and even began a competing cooking company for kids. This, I take full responsibility for because I saw the signs and chose to avoid reality. I chose to avoid uncomfortable conversations because I didn't want the added stress.

Growing this business has transformed me personally as much as it has professionally. In 2018, I attended a week-long Business Mastery Course hosted by the famous Tony Robbins. Upon returning from the training, I hired his coach for my personal journey and for my Tiny Chefs team in hopes that we would take the company to great heights.

What I began to discover was that I was the *only one* on the team committed to change. Most of them were afraid of any change or they simply didn't share the visions that I saw, which I now recognize are the values that I held. I was open to change because I saw the value of being open and self-exploratory. I knew my goals were expanding and was self-aware enough to know that I needed the coaching to fully obtain my goals. I began to realize that even though I had built a team around me that went above and beyond in their roles, they were not ready to explore personal development. This meant that I would have to approach how I trained them differently. Instead of pushing my agenda of coaching and personal development programs onto them, I set out to train them myself on how to communicate differently.

Surrender And Release

As time went on and my personal development journey expanded, my values began to shift and expand. I was feeling more and more comfortable in my own skin, therefore, things that I let slide before I was no longer able to do so. To my surprise, this *"new me"* didn't go over well with my Directors. Each time I applied pressure to support my values and beliefs, I was met with resistance. I was able to surrender my expectations and allow whatever happened to happen and be brave enough to let go of the result. I released my *"not good enough-ness,"* that need to be liked, and let caution fall to the wind.

There was both beauty and a curse in that I had nurtured the company in such a way that I could step away from day-to-day tasks. One of my goals was to work *on* my business not *in* my business. I knew that working in my business would prevent it from evolving from baby to toddler to adolescence to adult. It felt amazing and empowering to hand the reins over, however I came to realize that in doing so, I needed to have additional checks and balances in place, so to speak. Leaving most of the tasks into the hands of one Director meant that we had to have full transparency with one another, and this is never fully possible. What I learned through the ten years of employing three Directors, is that having an accountability system in place not only helps everyone feel seen and valued, but it keeps me accountable as well. I tended to believe that everything was going according to *"plan"* when in fact it wasn't.

Lead With Passion

One of the important techniques I learned which helped me lead my staff was the concept of wearing different hats. Since there are so many roles that are yours in the beginning, you must distinguish yourself accordingly. Wearing the kids cooking teacher hat is different from the training of your staff hat, especially when your role as staff trainer is to ensure people are educated in how you want your craft to be executed.

With experience comes familiarity with people and patterns. It's important to notice certain patterns in language, appearance, and mannerisms as quickly as possible so that you can hire and train the right people, not just *any* people. Quality control, I have found, should be the focus as an entrepreneur. That is because excellent quality is what is going to create the reputation that grows the company. Ultimately it is crucial to train the trainers efficiently because they need to be able to train the staff. The leadership role is to ensure that the little holes and gaps in the systems are getting plugged up and repaired as soon as they happen. It's also to assess and gather the failures and achievements to tweak the company based off the back of these experiences.

No one is going to care about your company like you do. Consider your company to be your infant baby who needs the utmost care and attention. All the details matter if you want it to grow into a healthy child, adolescent, and eventually, into an adult.

Grit And Grace

Through the pandemic I was fortunate enough to nurture Tiny Chefs in such a way that we stayed in the game. Many companies were closing their doors, but with the support of the government loans we were given the opportunity to shift our offerings to virtual cooking classes. It was during this time that I felt driven to start a new business as a women's empowerment coach. I created my company Anna Z Coaching and began to obtain certifications in NLP-Neuro Linguistic Programming and RTT-Rapid

Transformational Therapy. I was finally on my way to living my dream to help women become the best version of themselves in this lifetime. We all deserve to shine our brilliant light on ourselves and onto this world.

Coaching allowed me to teach once again, only this time, my purpose is to guide women to look inside themselves for their answers. I believe that we all have exactly what we need inside of us, we just need a mentor to help us see our light. The modalities that I work with provide such rapid transformation because I work with clearing out negative emotions and limiting beliefs in the subconscious mind. I believe that the challenges and experiences we have been given are there to create grit and grace. Grit makes us bad bitches and grace allows us to love ourselves that much more.

I have also developed, written, and executed courses so that I once again have a system in place. This is for greater outreach to help others. I truly feel blessed to have my dreams come true and in the order of which they did. My personal transformation has been parallel to my professional transformation and continues to this day.

Ignite Your Fire

What I know about mindset is that our reality is connected to what we believe. Our beliefs can make or break us, can hold us back or launch us into our truest version of self. We unlearn and unleash so we can expose our essence at the core. We peel back the layers so that we can begin again, this time we are the ones holding the reins. We feel into our knowing and use our inner compass to create our lives. We lead with our hearts.

Through my transformation, I've grown into the woman and powerhouse entrepreneur that I was born to be. Overnight success doesn't happen. It took over forty-eight years with the lessons and scars that helped me grow into my new reality. My fire was ignited, and my beliefs that drive me now are beliefs that help me keep the integrity of the business while valuing myself. I now know where my boundaries begin and end and where other's boundaries begin in relationship to mine. Everything is available to me and I'm here to show the world that when you hold yourself in high esteem, when you have self-love, self-trust, compassion, and joy, whatever you desire can be available to you. Ignite that fire in you!

Mastering others is strength.
Mastering yourself is true power.

Lao Tsu

Acknowledgments

LISA CARTER

Mom, thank you for always believing in me and never putting any limits on what you thought I could accomplish.

To my wonderful children, Robert, Kristina and Alycia. Each of you are so different, yet all three of you is what completes my heart. You are the fuel that keeps me moving forward. I am so proud of each and every one of you.

Ava and Claire, you taught me a whole new level of unconditional love. You are my world. I am so blessed to be your Mimi.

Ben, thank you for the being the 'crazy' glue that keeps us all together.

Lastly, Carol Starr Taylor from Star House Publishing Inc. for your guidance and support throughout this journey.

JULIE CRYNS

Thank you to my husband, Marke Jones, for his love and support.

Thank you to my children, Oliver and Savannah Cryns, for making me proud and loving me unconditionally, and to their dad, Mark Cryns, who lives on in our hearts.

Thank you to all the people who put their trust in me and allow me to guide them on their journey through grief.

PATI DIAZ

Thank you to my brother, Marcos, for being the one who always gets me and never making me feel judged.

To my sisters Mezlier, Jennifer, and Sandra for the dancing, singing, laughs, and love.

To my dad, Marcos, for always coming to get me no matter how far and for how long I wandered.

And to my mom, Lupe for passing on her love of travel and books and for always saying, "you should write."

DAWN ESPINOZA

To my parents, Bonnie and Ted, you know the sound of my heart and I yours, I am blessed.

To my children, Aliana and Davin, you are the reason I smile. I am "google, infinity and beyond" proud of you—Mom.

To my brothers, Kent and Terry, thank you for always being there for your little sister.

To Carol Starr Taylor, you are always my vibe and always in my tribe.

To my tribe, old friends and new, you keep me in a place of perpetual gratitude.

To you, dear reader, the light in me sees the light in you. May life's discoveries bring you full circle to slay your visions and your dreams.

ANNA GASPARI

I dedicate this book to the God that continues to grace with me with His love.

To my number one fan, the love of my life, my amazing husband, Mike. You are the greatest thing that has ever happened to me. Your support is immeasurable and I love you to infinity. Thank you for all that you do for me and our beautiful children!

JAMIE GATES

Thank you to my dad, Bill Gates, for being my rock and foundation and my bonus mom, Pam for loving me as her own.

To my daughter, Lynsie Law, who inspires me to be authentic and brave.

To my son, Jedidiah King, who challenges me to seek balance and live in grace.

To my boyfriend, Jeff Marks, for believing in me and pushing me to step out of my comfort zone.

To my tribe who uplifts and empowers me.

And to Sadie, the girl behind a flamingo named Sue.

CHRISTINE HENDERSON

I have so many people to thank for this amazing life I have!

To my family, for supporting me, even when I'm being stubborn.

To my staff over the last 25 years, thank you,

To the community of Bowmanville for always supporting my small business.

And most of all, to my husband Steve, who backs me up, no questions asked, at any cost, and gave up the life he knew to support my dream.

SANDRA LISI

Thank you is not enough to tell my biggest fans how grateful I am for their unconditional love and support throughout my life.

To my mom, dad and partner in life Elias; you are my pillar of strength, my rock and my circle of trust. I love you all.

Thank you to my friends, relationships, bosses (even the shitty ones), I learned from something from everyone. P.S. the shitty ones, they were the biggest teachers. They have all taught me something about myself and for that I thank them.

DR. KIM REDMAN

I would like to thank my dad who taught me to believe I could do anything. And to my husband Mike, who is my rock. *"In your eyes..."*

MICHELE MAHER

I wish to thank my parents JoAnne and Ted, for inspiring me to become the best version of myself, living with integrity and always having compassion for others.

To my sister Jennifer, for always being there for me.

To my beautiful children, Michael and Rachel, for introducing me to the concept of unconditional love. I hope you realize that you are capable of anything you put your mind to in life.

Acknowledgments

To my husband of more than 25 years, Leszek, thank you for putting up with me, and supporting me through all my entrepreneurial dreams.

MALI PHONPADITH

I would like to thank my husband, Victor Cora Nazario, my mother and father, Keonoukane and Sivone (in memoriam), my grandmother, Khamkong (in memoriam), Mina, Lola, Soudara, Ong, Lucy (my siblings), Luz (my mother-in-law), Victor (my father-in-law) (in memoriam), Hunter, Jaden, Reuben, Grace (my niece and nephews).

To my extended family, my dearest friends, mentors, guides and SOAR team, thank you for reminding me that my gifts, talents, mission and life's work are making a difference in our community. Let's continue to SOAR together!

ANNA ZECCOLO REEVES

I wish to thank the many people that I have worked with, for their vulnerability and for trusting me on their healing journey. It's their willingness to expand that helps us all expand.

To my creator, God, for the gift of life, and the challenges and opportunities I've been given to assist me in my evolution of self.

I thank, finally, my spirit guides who creatively and lovingly support me. I am forever grateful and feel cherished.

CPSIA information can be obtained
at www.ICGtesting.com
Printed in the USA
BVHW031346221122
652524BV00015B/615